Cambridge Elements

Elements in Digital Literary Studies
edited by
Katherine Bode
Australian National University
Adam Hammond
University of Toronto
Gabriel Hankins
Clemson University

DECOLONIAL DEEP MAPPING

Patricia Palmer
Maynooth University
Evan Bourke
Maynooth University
Philip Mac a' Ghoill
Maynooth University

Shaftesbury Road, Cambridge CB2 8EA, United Kingdom

One Liberty Plaza, 20th Floor, New York, NY 10006, USA

477 Williamstown Road, Port Melbourne, VIC 3207, Australia

314–321, 3rd Floor, Plot 3, Splendor Forum, Jasola District Centre, New Delhi – 110025, India

103 Penang Road, #05-06/07, Visioncrest Commercial, Singapore 238467

Cambridge University Press is part of Cambridge University Press & Assessment, a department of the University of Cambridge.

We share the University's mission to contribute to society through the pursuit of education, learning and research at the highest international levels of excellence.

www.cambridge.org
Information on this title: www.cambridge.org/9781009491846
DOI: 10.1017/9781009491853

© Patricia Palmer, Evan Bourke and Philip Mac a' Ghoill 2025

This publication is in copyright. Subject to statutory exception and to the provisions of relevant collective licensing agreements, no reproduction of any part may take place without the written permission of Cambridge University Press & Assessment.

When citing this work, please include a reference to the DOI 10.1017/9781009491853

First published 2025

A catalogue record for this publication is available from the British Library

ISBN 978-1-009-49184-6 Hardback
ISBN 978-1-009-49183-9 Paperback
ISSN 2633-4399 (online)
ISSN 2633-4380 (print)

Cambridge University Press & Assessment has no responsibility for the persistence or accuracy of URLs for external or third-party internet websites referred to in this publication and does not guarantee that any content on such websites is, or will remain, accurate or appropriate.

For EU product safety concerns, contact us at Calle de José Abascal, 56, 1°, 28003 Madrid, Spain, or email eugpsr@cambridge.org

Decolonial Deep Mapping

Elements in Digital Literary Studies

DOI: 10.1017/9781009491853
First published online: June 2025

Patricia Palmer
Maynooth University

Evan Bourke
Maynooth University

Philip Mac a' Ghoill
Maynooth University

Author for correspondence: Patricia Palmer, Pat.palmer@mu.ie

Abstract: Deep maps capture complex relationships to place and help trace the relationship between the abstract spaces of traditional maps and the cultural and literary history of the places that they represent. Using early modern Ireland as a template, this Element explores how deep-mapping techniques and a decolonial data ethic can be used to assemble a more culturally and linguistically representative archive and create more inclusive literary histories. It shows how deep mapping can disrupt colonial teleology and counter the monophone (and, specifically, anglophone) colonial record by bringing the long-neglected voices of the colonised back into the conversation. In doing so, it recovers a pre-conquest cultural vibrancy which colonisation, the language shift from Irish to English, and scholarly inattention successively occluded. More broadly, it offers a model for engaging with decolonial literary deep maps by developing reading strategies for 'juxtapuntal' reading that has the potential to decolonise the canon.

Keywords: digital humanities, literary geographies, literary peripheries, early modern Ireland, comparative eco-criticism

© Patricia Palmer, Evan Bourke and Philip Mac a' Ghoill 2025

ISBNs: 9781009491846 (HB), 9781009491839 (PB), 9781009491853 (OC)
ISSNs: 2633-4399 (online), 2633-4380 (print)

Contents

1. Countering Colonial Cartography and Coloniality — 1
2. Developing a Decolonial Literary Deep Map — 15
3. Decolonial Reading Strategies: Archives, Contiguity, and the Juxtapuntal — 30
4. Juxtapuntal Readings: Mapping Counter-Discourses — 50
5. Coda — 67

Bibliography — 71

1 Countering Colonial Cartography and Coloniality

Colonialism has a long afterlife. If we are lucky, we live among its ruins, building independent republics out of the detritus of empire.[1] If we are not, we live amid the inequalities and violence left in its wake. *Si monumentum requiris circumspice*; if you want to see its legacy, just look around: the afterlife of conquest, dispossession, and settlement is still playing out in conflicts that bedevil the present. In 1972, the bloodiest year of 'The Troubles' in Northern Ireland,[2] John Montague published *The Rough Field*. Through a bricolage that samples and re-contextualises colonial texts and images, Montague reflects on the conflict by going back to its origins, the Nine Years War (1593–1603) and the Plantation of Ulster (1609 ff.). Montague finds that bitter colonial history written on the landscape, both in the transformative – terra-formative – land practices of empire and in the process of anglicisation which had made familiar place(name)s strange:

> The whole landscape a manuscript
> We had lost the skill to read,
> A part of our past disinherited.[3]

The past offered Brian Friel, too, a way of understanding – and intervening in – the present. The emotional resonance of his play *Translations* (1980) comes from Friel's intuition that cartography, by overwriting autochthonous narratives of place, is a metonym for colonisation more generally. Not alone did colonial mapping supply the working documents for 'alienating', in a legal sense, the land from its hereditary occupiers, it also set in motion a chain of dispossession that was emotionally, epistemologically, and imaginatively alienating as well. For Friel, cartography and, in his case, the Ordinance Survey of the 1820s, captured the ruptures and violent after-shocks of conquest, dispossession, and plantation. Friel's mapping metaphors turn increasingly elegiac. Hugh, the head-schoolmaster, fatalistically concedes that 'a civilization can be imprisoned in a linguistic contour which no longer matches the landscape of ... fact'.[4] By the end, the lights are going down on a world whose time is understood to be up, and on a language – or, if we add Latin to Irish, two languages – rendered archaic and redundant by the new colonial order.

---

[1] In Ireland, the repurposing has sometimes been quite literal: gaols, barracks, and military hospitals (the Royal Barracks, Kilmainham Gaol, the Royal Hospital) now house museums and galleries.
[2] CAIN Archive: Conflict and Politics in Northern Ireland: www.cain.ulster.ac.uk/index.html.
[3] John Montague, 'A Lost Tradition', Section IV, A Severed Head, in *The Rough Field* (Oldcastle: Gallery Press, 1972).
[4] Brian Friel, *Translations*, p.52.

This Element asks whether there is a way of requiting colonial cartography with something other than elegy. It explores how we might respond to the univocality of colonial mapping with another form of mapping – deep mapping – that challenges the distortions and exclusions of a practice rooted in military conquest, colonisation, and a sustained campaign of turning land into property. Deep mapping opens the possibility of recovering polyphony, of re-admitting what was once excluded, because it is, as David Bodenhamer notes, 'a medium that encourages multiplicity, competing perspectives, and alternative worldviews'.[5] Rather than simply supplying an Irish *verso* to the English *recto* of the original maps, and thereby replaying the black-and-white logic of colonialism, we want to make available a multifariousness that exceeds the tit-for-tat play of binary thinking. What happened in early modern Ireland was not just a conflict around land, ethnicity, and religion (though it was all of those); it was also a multilayered contest of meanings, values, and orientations to the world. The deep map featured in this Element is one of two visualisations created by the MACMORRIS Project (the other is a network interface). Funded by the Irish Research Council,[6] MACMORRIS (Mapping Actors and Communities: Modelling Research in Renaissance Ireland in the Sixteenth and Seventeenth Century) is a digital humanities project which seeks to create an inclusive account of creative, scholarly, and intellectual activity, across cultures, ethnicities, and languages, from 1541 to 1660. It encompasses, therefore, the successive phases of the Tudor, Stuart, and Cromwellian conquest of Ireland. Like the rest of the project, the deep map was undertaken with decolonising intent; in following that intention to its logical conclusion, we come to see that what was ultimately being colonised everywhere in early modernity was the earth itself.

1.1 Mapping Plantation and Dispossession

The aim of the MACMORRIS deep map is to restore what the colonial maps – and the wider processes they enabled – silenced. Moreover, given that scholarship on early modern Ireland continues to draw disproportionately on colonial sources, it has the further aim of expanding and pluralising the archive. For our case study, we chose Munster, Ireland's southern province. Broad majestic rivers flow through some of the richest land in Europe. Its port towns, Waterford, Cork, Berehaven, Limerick, traded with south-east England and the Atlantic Arc, and its fishing grounds were among the most bountiful in Europe. '[I]f there be any countrey that Floweth wth mylk and honie this

---

[5] Bodenhamer, 'Narrating Space and Place', pp.7–27, p.18.
[6] Project Reference: IRCLA/2019/116. For a fuller account of MACMORRIS, see www.macmorris.maynoothuniversity.ie/#about-us and Palmer, 'Making MACMORRIS'. https://mural.maynoothuniversity.ie/19257/.

province is one of them', the mapmaker, Francis Jobson, declared, having spent three years surveying it.[7] This was a hybridised society where the descendants of the twelfth-century Anglo-Normans (the 'Old English') had assimilated and intermarried with the Gaelic Irish without entirely losing their cultural distinctiveness. The Tudors' reassertion of a territorial claim to Ireland, the imposition of Protestantism as the state religion, and freelance attempts to establish new colonies all provoked resistance, culminating in two Desmond Wars (1569–1573, 1579–1583). The beheading of the Earl of Desmond in 1583 ended a bloody conflict in which many as 50,000 people died.[8] The scorched-earth policy which Edmund Spenser, among others, advocated – took its intended toll.[9] What was left was a wasteland stalked by death and the colonial dream of a *terra nullius* ripe for the plantation:

> the numbers of them are infinit, whose blouds the earth dranke vp, and whose carcases the foules of the aire and the rauening beasts of the féeld did consume and deuoure. After this folowed an extreme famine: and such as whom the sword did not destroie, the same did consume, and eat out; verie few or none remaining alive ... everie waie the cursse of God was so great, and the land so barren both of man and beast, that whosoeuer did trauell from the one end vnto the other of all Mounster, euen from *Waterford* to the head of Sméerewéeke, which is about six score miles, he should not meet anie man, woman, or child, sauing in townes and cities; nor yet sée anie beast, but the verie woolues, the foxes, and other like rauening beasts: manie of them laie dead being famished, and the residue gone elsewhere.[10]

Roughly 580,000 English acres, escheated from the Desmonds and their confederates, became available to the Crown for replanting with loyal English settlers.

Maps – the colonial maps that the MACMORRIS deep map counters – played a key role at every stage of the conquest and the plantation that followed. It is to three of these maps that we now turn. Each has its own opacities and blindspots. But, both in what they included and what they omitted and silenced, they provided a framework for the MACMORRIS deep map. What was on the colonial map would offer a provocation – and what was off it, a purchase – for the deep map. The first of the three is Robert Lythe's 'Single draght of Mounster' (see Figure 1),[11] drawn in the winter of 1571 for the Lord Deputy, Sir

---

[7] Jobson, 'The Province of Munster'. [8] Smyth, *Map-Making*, p.47.
[9] Spenser proposed driving 'the enemie ... from one steade to another, and tennis him amongst them', while stampeding, starving, and killing the cattle that sustained them: 'one winters well followinge of him will soe plucke him on his knees, that he will never be able to stand up againe'. Edmund Spenser, *A View of the Present State of Ireland*, p.98.
[10] Most of the contemporary sources quoted in this Element come, as here, from the deep map. www.macmorris.maynoothuniversity.ie/site/203.
[11] TNA MPF 1/73.

Figure 1 Robert Lythe's 'Single draght of Mounster', TNA MPF 1/73 (Courtesy of The National Archives, Kew).

Henry Sidney. Sidney knew the value of maps in advancing the conquest and, from 1567 to 1571, he brought Lythe with him on campaign. Sidney's 'magical' mapmaker[12] delivered detailed and accurate topographical intelligence. Charting the south-west coast, with its endless involutions of inlets and islands, from the pinnace of a warship, he uncovers how many 'Fateme deape' a haven is at 'low-water' and where 'Great Shyps' will have sufficient draught to come close to shore. Most strikingly, however, this is a map of names. Everywhere, topography is overwritten by toponymy: Lythe's crabbed handwriting records (in black) the names of towns, rivers, islands, mountains, sounds, and headlands. He labels the old territorial divisions (e.g. 'Carbre') in purple ink and the names of the Gaelic and Old English lords in red. The words 'Sr Owen

---

[12] Klein, *Maps and the Writing of Space in Early Modern England and Ireland*, p.64. On Sidney's centrality to the conquest, see Canny, *Elizabethan Conquest*.

Oswyllyuant Beare' are slashed, north-south, across the neck of the Beare peninsula, while 'Baron of lyxnay' fits into the gentle undulations of the Stack's Mountains. The titling of lords by their territory and the inscription of their names onto the map – 'Erle of Dysmond', 'Oconer Kerey', 'knyght of the valley' – literalise the coincidence of identity and territory that characterised Gaelic lordships. Lythe's naming of hereditary lords, large and small, is 'exceptional ... in West European mapping but not in the wider imperial context'.[13] But even as he records the hereditary septs and their territories, he is also inscribing the boundaries of a new administrative order. New, carefully coloured-in county boundaries answer to Sidney's determination to root out the territorial organisation of the kinship-based system of lordship and turn Ireland into 'shire ground'.[14]

But for all that Lythe's map is an accessory to conquest – it is commissioned as a military field map by a ruthless commander – its meanings exceed its intended function. That cartographic 'excess' offers a starting point for decolonial deep mapping. Lythe's map encodes more stories than he himself could access, and those gaps in the telling create a space for decolonial deep mapping. True, in reducing Irish-language placenames to a rubble of phonemes – all those 'slews' and 'knocks' and 'cans'[15] – the map marks an early stage in the systematic anglicisation of Ireland. But transliteration, unlike the pattern of erasure and renaming characteristic of plantation,[16] retains a semantic base that can still be activated. Lythe may turn Mullach Allaíre into 'Mollocghalerre' but its meaning, 'summit of the partial deafness or echo', still echoes through its tone-deaf transliteration.[17] As we shall see in the Coda, even such distortions offer passage to a much more intimate knowledge of place, stored in the placename lore of *Dindseanchas*. Equally, while the names of lords plastered across Lythe's map serve to identify antagonists in a colonial gameplan, their inscription is, nonetheless, an acknowledgement of prior occupancy. Their presence constitutes an unintended chthonic assertion, much like the sketch of three warrior figures who seem to rise out of the earth itself, in the north-west of John Goghe's 'Map of Ireland' (1567). Indeed, it was the rich suggestion of an antecedent, telluric presence challenging the univocality of the colonial map that led us to select one of those figures for the MACMORRIS logo (see Figure 2).[18]

---

[13] Smyth, *Map-making*, p.38; see also p.82. [14] Canny, *Elizabethan Conquest*, p.52.
[15] *Recte* 'sliabh', mountain, 'cnoc', hill, 'cenn', head.
[16] The Settlement of Laois and Offaly Act of 1556, for example, conjured up 'Queen's' and 'King's' counties, and their respective county towns, Maryborough (now Portlaoise) and Philipstown (now Daingean) from the Gaelic kingdoms of Loígis and Uí Failghe.
[17] Placenames Database of Ireland: www.logainm.ie/en/11901. [18] TNA MPF1/68.

Figure 2 MACMORRIS logo.

Fifteen years after Lythe ruined his eyesight completing his map,[19] Desmond and his allies were defeated. Their land was confiscated by the Crown; their names could be razed from the map. In planning the transfer of escheated lands to English settlers, Lord Burleigh pored over a much more schematic map, the 'Plot of the attainted lands and how the same is allocated to the undertakers' (1586) (see Figure 3).[20] Here, after the devastation of the Desmond Wars, Munster, apart from its orientalised cities, is a blank, stripped of features and inhabitants. Here we see what Robert Sack, in *Human Territoriality*, calls the 'emptiable space' of [early] capitalism.[21] This, it seems, is an unpeopled *terra nullius* ripe for the taking – and Lord Burleigh's hand-written notes on the map catch Elizabeth I's Chief Secretary in the act of divvying out the seignories to English petitioners. The western extremity of this inviting *tabula rasa*, for example, is filled in with a promissory note: 'The County of Kerry' is 'Desired by Sir William Harbart'.

The sequel is written all over our third map, Francis Jobson's 'Province of Munster' (see Figure 4), which he sent to Burleigh, on 30 May 1589. The map gave the plantation's architect a snapshot of it bedding down. In the Trinity College Dublin copy, Jobson's letter dedicatory flanks both sides of the map. Jobson tells Burleigh that he 'shall finde' the different seignories, 'circumferensed and distinguished the on[e] from the other wth lines of carnation color with the names of everie vndertaker to who*m* such parcells are allotted written w^{t}h^{in} the said particulares in Romaine text'.[22] A massive 'RAWLLE' stamps the 40,000 acres, stretching from Youghal to Lismore, granted to Sir Walter. 'Kilcolman' marks the more modest, 4000-acre seignory conferred on Edmund Spenser. And, as an update to Burleigh's annotation on the 1586 blank map, the map shows that Sir William Herbert did indeed receive what he 'desired': 'HARBART' is splashed across a swathe of land centred on the 'Illand of Kerry'. The two royal coats of arms at the top of the map and the six galleons flying the flag of St George painted on the stippled sea around Munster flatteringly suggest that, here, England rules land and sea. Like Lythe, Jobson draws in the new shire boundaries, explaining that he 'distingwyshed the counties contained w^{thin} the said province the one from the other wth a chained line'. Jobson's choice of a concatenation of chain links – the mapmaker's measuring 'lines' – to demarcate the administrative

---

[19] Andrews, 'The Irish Surveys of Robert Lythe', 22–31, 26.
[20] TNA MPF 1/273, 17 June 1586, Extracted Maps and Plans.
[21] Sack, *Human Territoriality*, p.48.   [22] IE TCD MS 1209/36.

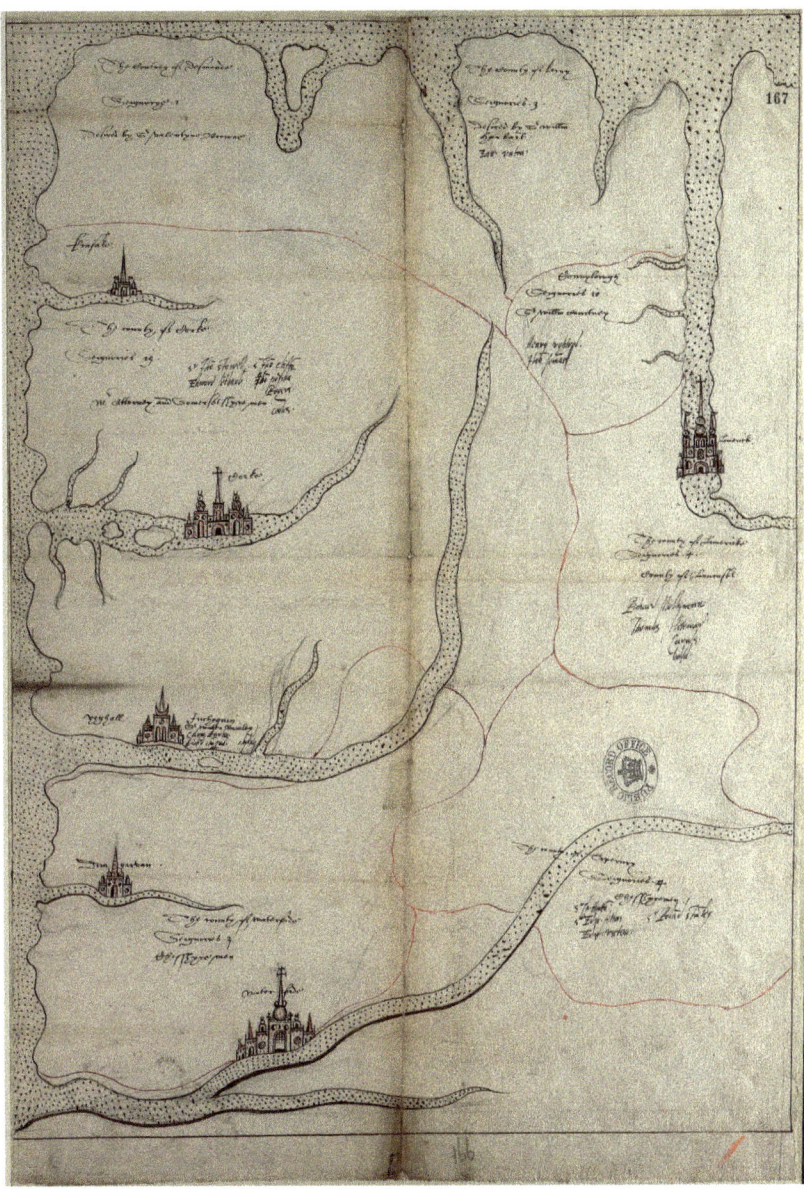

Figure 3 'Plot of the attainted lands and how the same is allocated to the undertakers', TNA MPF 1/273, 17 June 1586, Extracted Maps and Plans (Courtesy of The National Archives, Kew).

units of a new colonial order literalises the way cartography and conquest marched in link step, 'enclos[e]ing Ireland within tighter grids of rule'.[23]

---
[23] Smyth, *Map-Making*, p.38.

Figure 4 Francis Jobson's 'Province of Munster', IE TCD MS 1209/36 (Courtesy of Trinity College Dublin).

1.2 Countering the Colonial Map

'[F]ar from being pictures of the world', Dennis Wood reminds us, 'maps are instruments for its creation; that is, they are not representations but systems of propositions, arguments about what the world might be.'[24] Historically, those propositions were colonial and extractive. The foundational map of Nigeria, for example, was produced by the Intelligence Division of the British War Office in 1901, hot on the heels of the Crown's acquisition of the Southern and Northern Nigeria Protectorate from the Royal Niger Company; it came in useful in the campaign of conquest which followed. Most subsequent maps of Africa's largest country were made by oil- and gas-exploration companies or external-state actors.[25] From the late 1980s, cartography's historical indentureship to

---

[24] Wood, *Rethinking the Power of Maps*, p.8.
[25] 'Nigeria – Gas and Oil', a map of oil- and gas-fields, pipelines, refineries, and tanker terminals made by the CIA, brings together those twinned (neo)colonial and extractive impulses; see Map

power – state power, the power of capital, and their mutual entanglement – provided rich pickings for critical geography, given its 'alertness to the multiple and imbricated geographies through which oppression and domination are produced'.[26] Critical cartographers like J. B. Hartley, who saw maps as 'primarily a form of political discourse concerned with the acquisition and maintenance of power', explored how their distortions and silences worked to produce 'a visual language communicating proprietorial or territorial rights in both practical and symbolic senses'.[27] Some critical geographers, moreover, were keen to go beyond critique, seeking 'to use (geographic) data to unite critical ideas and radical practice to explore and realize more equitable alternative possibilities'.[28] Counter-mapping presented itself as one way 'to effect change not only through transformative insight but also through forms of progressive praxis'.[29]

Counter-mapping emerged as one response to that desire for real-world intervention. It supplements 'critical scholarship ... with situated, reflexive practice', opening up 'a promising avenue for a critically aware data science dedicated to creating new worlds'.[30] It becomes one of the ways in which 'decolonizing actually occurs in practice'.[31] Jeremy Crampton defines what he calls 'critical mapping' or 'critical GIS' (and which we, following Nancy Peluso, call 'counter-mapping') as any mapping project 'which has an activist, emancipatory flavor to it'.[32] Harris and Hazen define counter-mapping as 'any effort that fundamentally questions the assumptions or biases of cartographic conventions, that challenges predominant power effects of mapping, or that engages in mapping in ways that upset power relations'.[33] Moreover, it does so in a way that is 'creative [and] multitudinal': 'counter-mapping mixes theory and practice to be *productive* and *generative*, a way to open, explore, and realize alternatives to the status quo.'[34]

The map with which this Element is principally concerned – a deep map of an Irish province in the later sixteenth century – may seem worlds (and several centuries) away from counter-mapping's urgent engagement with the present. Yet, in a genealogy that blurs the boundary between a counter-map of a present

---

No. 504014 1979, Perry-Castañeda Library Map Collection, University of Texas at Austin: www.maps.lib.utexas.edu/maps/nigeria.html.
[26] Blomley, 'Uncritical Critical Geography?' 87–94, 89.
[27] Hartley, 'Silences and Secrecy', 57–76, 57, 59; see also 'Deconstructing the Map', 1–20.
[28] Dalton and Stallmann, 'Counter-Mapping', 93–101, 94.
[29] Blomley, 'Uncritical Critical Geography?' 91–92.
[30] Dalton and Stallmann, 'Counter-Mapping', 100.
[31] Oslender, 'Decolonizing Cartography and Ontological Conflict', 1–12, 2.
[32] Crampton, *Mapping*, p.17. See Peluso, 'Whose Woods?' 383–406.
[33] Harris and Hazen, 'The Power of Maps', 99–130, 115.
[34] Dalton and Stallmann, 'Counter-Mapping', 94; emphasis in original.

emergency and a deep map of a past conflict, the origin story of the MACMORRIS deep map lies in a counter-mapping project in the Niger Delta. For MACMORRIS, the continuum between counter-mapping and deep-mapping exists for the simple reason that there is a continuum between early modernity and the modernity which it constituted and in which we still live. A through line runs from early modern *colonialism* to present-day *coloniality*. Anibal Quijano originated the concept of the 'coloniality of power' to trace the direct lineage from colonialism to coloniality. Coloniality, in Quijano's analysis, is a world system that reproduces and continues to profit from racial, political, and social inequalities instituted by colonisation.[35] The 'depth' of our deep map comes, in part, from that dual temporality – the 'then' of colonialism and the 'now' of coloniality – and from the belief that to challenge propositions posited as 'verities' in early modernity is, at the same time, to challenge successor propositions that continue to power the destructive logics of inequality and extraction in the present. To counter-map the past is, inescapably, to intervene in the present.

The map that laid the intellectual foundations for the MACMORRIS deep map was a counter-map of informal settlements in Port Harcourt, Nigeria's oil capital. Over half a million people live in the city's forty-nine informal waterfront settlements. These are largely self-built communities lacking any form of municipal infrastructure: no sewerage systems, no state health services, no formal engagement with government. The settlements are built on land that the residents themselves reclaimed from the creeks, by blending estuarine mud ('chicoco') with refuse. They lie between five and fifteen metres lower than the rest of the city, which is sited on a laterite plateau, creating a physical marker of their spatial and social segregation. In 2009, Governor Amaechi of Rivers State, availing of a 1978 land-use decree issued by the military junta vesting all urban land in trust to the governor, announced plans to demolish the informal waterfront settlements. These settlements did not exist on any municipal map. They featured on the city's development plan only as undifferentiated zones marked for demolition – and soon the bulldozers were moving in. Michael Uwemedimo, an English literature lecturer with a camera, filmed the demolitions for Amnesty International.[36] Uwemedimo joined community activists to set up an arts-advocacy NGO, Collaborative Media Advocacy Platform (CMAP).[37]

---

[35] Quijano, 'Coloniality of Power, Eurocentrism, and Latin America', 215–32.

[36] www.cmapping.net/they-came-with-their-bulldozers-they-came-with-their-soldiers/.

[37] As well as mapping, that included documentary filmmaking for advocacy and legal purposes and setting up a radio station, Chicoco FM, and developing content, to give voice to the community: www.cmapping.net/communicating-and-campaigning www.amnesty.org/en/latest/news/2014/06/nigeria-slum-dwellers-victory-over-government-international-court-triumph-against-impunity/.

At that time, Uwemedimo was collaborating with Pat Palmer, later the principal investigator of the MACMORRIS project, on a knowledge-exchange programme with King's College London.[38] One of its strands was to develop a pedagogy that could explore how ideologies of colonialism, property, extraction, violence, and racialisation to which canonical texts from the first, early modern phase of English colonial expansion gave expression could be brought into conversation both with texts from later imperial moments and with the continuing afterlife of colonialism now.[39] When the demolitions started, we were confronted with a crisis that exemplified the double timeframe we had been exploring in the classroom. Here was the legacy of British colonialism playing out in one of coloniality's most damnified 'undersides' (to borrow Enrique Dussel's term).[40] Academic reflections on 'representation' ceded to the need to represent the waterfront communities cartographically. Theoretical discussions around the need to 'draft maps of the visible' turned literal.[41]

Although almost half a million people lived in Port Harcourt's informal waterfront settlements, they were off the map. To make them visible in a way that was legible to government officials, CMAP embarked on a participatory mapping project.[42] In actions that echo Nancy Peluso's definition of counter mapping, they set about 'challenging the omissions of human settlements from maps, for contesting the homogenization of space on political, zoning, or property maps'.[43] Local volunteers were trained to use QGIS mapping software. In parallel, the wider community was introduced to the practice and benefits of participatory mapping through a radio drama, 'Map my Soup'.[44] The resultant survey produced maps that are extraordinarily rich in data. Geo-referenced points contain data about topography, land use, building type, and use. Following the initial mapping, community mappers returned to every house and business, to collect information about population, tenure, employment, governance, and access to health and education. To supplement this quantitative data, volunteers took photographs and recorded interviews to story-map life on the waterfront. A publicity campaign, 'People Live Here', ran alongside the mapping project. Bus wraps with portraits of individual waterfront residents gave a disregarded community visibility on the streets of official Port Harcourt.[45] The survey data itself is owned by the residents and once it was

---

[38] For details, see www.kcl.ac.uk/cultural/projects/2017/reimagining-the-city and www.kcl.ac.uk/cultural/assets/160407-workshop-report-4-nov-2015.pdf.
[39] Palmer, 'Another Past Was Possible'. [40] Dussel, *The Underside of Modernity.*
[41] Rancière, *The Politics of Aesthetics*, p. 39.
[42] www.cmapping.net/building-and-planning/chicoco-maps. [43] Peluso, 'Whose Woods?' 387.
[44] Listen here: www.soundcloud.com/chicoco-radio/many-voices-make-a-city-2.
[45] www.people-live-here.org/.

amassed the waterfront communities moved to proposition. They drew up a People's Plan that brought planners, politicians, and ordinary people from across Port Harcourt together, to produce 'appropriate urban development models, and ... a needs-based, rights-protective urban plan'.[46] CMAP's work encapsulates Dalton and Stallmann's definition of counter mapping 'as a straightforward tactic for confronting asymmetrical power relations, as a kind of linguistic proposition, and as an intentionally creative, practiced social formation',[47] and it is still playing out.

The unbroken line between colonisation and coloniality is patiently obvious in the crisis to which CMAP responded. (Inevitably, the training of the volunteer mappers included a section on colonial cartography.) Counter-mapping is usually *countering* historical and often colonial patterns of dispossession and exploitation. For example, the counter-maps created by people in Kalimantan, Borneo, to assert their territorial forest rights, on which Nancy Peluso worked, challenge extractive logics, notions of ownership and territorialisation, and the abrogation of Dayak customary rights that have their origins in sixteenth-century Dutch colonisation.[48] MACMORRIS's deep map flips counter-mapping's temporal focus. Instead of intervening in a present outgrowth of historical injustices, it focuses on the past that shaped the present. The 'depth' in the MACMORRIS deep map comes, in part, from a double time frame, rooted in its awareness that what happened in early modernity did not stay in early modernity. Early modernity, rather, determined our modernity; it continues to dictate our present, and its propositions and practices threaten our future. Our flipped focus was also a split focus. That concentration on the early modern 'then' of colonialism while staying attentive to the 'now' of coloniality is an important element in making it a *decolonial* deep map.

That double time frame is activated by the texts on the deep map. Drawn, roughly, from the last three decades of the sixteenth century and the first decade of the seventeenth, these texts bring us to the upheaval of a traditional society being upended by conquest and colonisation. The texts of those advancing the conquest articulate the violence, justifications, and extractive purpose of a new, expansionist colonial order. Gaelic texts sometimes resist those propositions or voice countervailing propositions; more often and more valuably, they bring us to perspectives and world views entirely outside the inchoate but protean discourses of conquest and colonisation. What is emerging – and being contested – live on the deep map is, in miniature, nothing less than the emergence of discourses of control, of nature-as-resource, of racialisation, of rationalised violence that still

---

[46] www.cmapping.net/building-and-planning/towards-a-peoples-plan.
[47] Dalton and Stallmann, 'Counter-Mapping', 96.
[48] On the historical prequel, see Ghosh, *The Nutmeg's Curse*.

haunt the present, in the form of coloniality. 'The conceptualization of modernity/ coloniality', Arturo Escobar explains, involved precisely this two-step process: 'a hegemonic representation and mode of knowing that claims universality for itself' and the 'subalternization of the knowledge and cultures' of those 'outside the European core'.[49] If colonisation operated by imposing its own local imperatives and self-interested values on others, declaring them 'universal', and then minoritised the languages and epistemologies of the colonised, its successor, coloniality, cashes in on those manoeuvers by insisting there is no alternative to its 'universals' and globalising them. Given their hegemony at the end of that long process, where, Arturo Escobar asks, can 'radical alterity' come from?[50] Where do we find something 'exterior' to 'the modern world system'? 'Exteriority' is an important concept and, as Escobar is careful to point out, it 'does not entail an ontological outside; it refers to an outside that is precisely constituted as difference by a hegemonic discourse'. It is to be found, in part, in what coloniality makes exterior to itself – the poor, the racialised, the indigenous, nature itself.[51] Finding critical perspectives exterior to coloniality entails

> the rescuing of non-hegemonic and silenced counter-discourses, of the alterity that is constitutive of modernity itself. This is the ethical principle of liberation of the negated Other, for which Dussel coins the term, 'transmodernity', defined as a project for overcoming modernity not simply by negating it but by thinking about it from its underside, from the perspective of the excluded other.[52]

Walter Mignolo, likewise seeking an exteriority from which critique can be mounted, uses Gloria Anzaldúa's concept of 'border thinking' to suggest that the challenge must come from the edge, from what has been made peripheral. It will require 'thinking from an other place, imagining an other language, arguing from an other logic'. Mignolo calls this kind of thinking 'pluritopic [multi-place] hermeneutics'.[53] But, we argue, that the critique can come from another *time* as well as another *place*. So, to Mignolo's 'pluritopic hermeneutics' we would add a 'pluri-*chronic*' dimension, a critique that reintroduces what was subalternised in the past and which colonialism needed to make 'exterior' precisely so that modernity could take the shape it did. Perspectives that had to be repressed so that colonialism could thrive encode ideas still capable of commenting aslant on coloniality.

---

[49] Escobar, 'Worlds and Knowledges Otherwise, 179–210, 184.
[50] Escobar, 'Worlds and Knowledges Otherwise', 181.
[51] Escobar, 'Worlds and Knowledges Otherwise', 186.
[52] Escobar, 'Worlds and Knowledges Otherwise', 187.
[53] See Mignolo, *The Darker Side of the Renaissance* and *Local Histories/Global Designs*, p.313.

In his analysis of how critical mapping and critical GIS can challenge hegemonic orders of knowledge, Crampton suggests that 'one way … is by putting them into historical perspective. This historicization of knowledge not only shows that other times did things differently, but by providing an intellectual history it allows us to see the edges of our own limits, and to conceive of other knowledges that might be useful'.[54] The MACMORRIS deep map provides just such a 'historicization of knowledge'. Deep mapping is all about providing a platform for multiplicity. The affordances of the deep map chime perfectly, therefore, with the need to bring perspectives exterior to the 'universals' of colonisation/coloniality – 'the alterity that is constitutive of modernity itself'[55] face to face with the colonial discourses which excluded them. Deep mapping enables two of the strategies that Mignolo identifies as instrumental in the project of decolonialising, 'border thinking' and 'pluriversality'. Border thinking 'sees decolonization as a particular kind of deconstruction but moves towards a fragmented, plural project instead of reproducing the abstract universals of modernity'.[56] 'Pluriversality' entails 'viewing the world as an interconnected diversity'. Whereas '[u]niversality is always imperial and war driven, [p]luri- and multiverses are convivial, dialogical, or plurilogical'.[57] 'Fragmented', 'plural', 'diverse', 'convivial', 'dialogical', 'plurilogical': these are also the signatures of deep mapping. Form and function fuse in the decolonial deep map.

One question remains: What is Ireland doing here? Many of the ideas shaping our practice come from coloniality's 'underside'. Already, we have drawn examples and theory from Nigeria, Indonesia, and Latin America. Our own situatedness in a country that hovers around the top of most international economic rankings, therefore, needs some explaining. Uncritical celebration of Ireland's 'postcolonial' status, and the moral clarity imagined to be inherent to that condition, often conveniently overlooks its current imbrication in the web of coloniality. To make recourse to Ireland in seeking to challenge coloniality, therefore, requires that we recognise the country's anomalous double positioning. Ireland was colonised in early modernity. Successive plantations in the sixteenth and seventeenth century transferred 73 per cent of the land of Ireland to settler colonists.[58] But, out of a painful history that encompasses the Great Hunger, depopulation, violent struggle, and post-independence stagnation, Ireland transitioned from colony to postcolonial hub within capitalism's globalised, neoliberal coloniality of power. (In the same way as the wretched of the earth fleeing famine in Ireland transitioned into becoming settler colonists in

---

[54] Crampton, *Mapping*, p. 17. [55] Escobar, 'Worlds and Knowledges Otherwise', 187.
[56] Escobar, 'Worlds and Knowledges Otherwise', 206.
[57] Mignolo, 'Foreword', p.xi, p.x, p.xii.
[58] Siochrú and Brown, 'The Down Survey and the Cromwellian Land Settlement', p. 606.

lands dispossessed from others.)[59] *Post*colonial but hardly *de*colonial, Ireland itself needs the lessons made available by mapping its pre/colonial past more than most. Equally, by exploring the processes of violence, exclusion, and replacement through which its modernity was constituted – a modernity piloted in Ireland which would later be exported worldwide – early modern Ireland and its chiastic successor, modern Ireland, between them have much to reveal about the constructedness of – and therefore the possibility of reconstructing – the present settlement. After all, as Robertson and Mullen argue, and this Element attempts to demonstrate, '[d]eep maps are the first part of imagining something different.'[60]

2 Developing a Decolonial Literary Deep Map

The philosopher Jeff Malpas argues that 'place is perhaps the key term for interdisciplinary research in the arts, humanities and social sciences in the twenty-first century'.[61] This is because 'place is not just a thing in the world but a way of understanding the world'. For Tim Cresswell, place is

> how we make the world meaningful and the way we experience the world. Place, at a basic level, is space invested with meaning in the context of power. This process of investing space with meaning happens across the globe at all scales, and has done throughout human history.[62]

The central premise of this Element is that deep-mapping techniques capture complex relationships to place and help to trace the relationship between the abstract spaces of traditional maps and the cultural and literary history of the places which they represent. As Robertson and Mullen point out, the adjective 'deep' implies multiplicity,[63] and that depth is achieved by layering multiple textual, visual, and multimedia artefacts together. That multiplicity allows the deep map to reproduce the 'pluriversality' which Mignolo identifies with decolonial praxis. Moreover, deep mapping allows us to play with time as well as place. That double valence makes deep maps particularly suitable for decolonial counter-mapping strategies that challenge the 'then' of colonialism and the 'now' of coloniality. This synergy enables a re-evaluation of the

---

[59] As Eve Tuck and K. Wayne Yang sternly remind us, 'Settlers are not immigrants. Immigrants are beholden to the Indigenous laws and epistemologies of the lands they migrate to. Settlers become the law, supplanting Indigenous laws and epistemologies'; in 'Decolonization Is Not a Metaphor', 1–40, 6–7.
[60] Robertson and Mullen, 'Navigating through Narrative', p.134.
[61] www.progressivegeographies.com/2010/11/04/place-research-network/.
[62] Cresswell, *Place*, p.19.
[63] Robertson and Mullen, 'Navigating through Narrative', p.133; www.cliffordmclucas.info/deep-mapping.html.

knowledge produced in colonial contexts and can enable the recovery, restoration, and restitution of sources and perspectives that are 'subalternised' in dominant colonial literary historiographies. The aim of this section is to present a decolonial praxis for deep mapping and to explore how the MACMORRIS deep map facilitates multiperspectival and pluriversal interrogations of events, places, texts, and concepts.

2.1 What Is Literary Deep Mapping?

Deep maps help trace the relationship between the abstract space we see on a traditional map and the cultural history of places. Some do this by employing GIS software, which Charles Travis argues acts as a 'platform upon which to cartographically collate and visualize various layers of historical narrative'.[64] But, the act of making a deep map 'is more than a matter of applying GIS and related geospatial tools, no matter how central the technology may be in constructing the map itself'.[65] Bodenhamer lists the characteristics of a deep map: it is flexible, invites exploration; it is 'user-centric', presents different views, support narration; it's impressive and it evokes experience.[66] Nicholas Bauch reminds us that deep maps 'do not operate under the belief that objective reality is being recreated'; instead, they implicitly prompt 'multiple responses'.[67] Imogen Humphris, Lummina G. Horlings, and Iain Biggs argue that deep maps offer

> opportunities to generate representations that 'dive into' the heterogeneity and non-aligned multiplicity of place ... Deep maps embrace, as their starting point, the tensions that exist between incompatible narratives and between one slice of time and the next. They seek to draw out those discordant, micro-narratives that are commonly swallowed up within meta-narratives of a place.[68]

Clifford McLucas emphasises that deep maps 'will not seek the authority and objectivity of conventional cartography. They will be politicized, passionate, and partisan. They will involve negotiation and contestation over who and what is represented and how'.[69] Overall, deep maps simultaneously aid in and complicate explorations of place. By foregrounding complex relationships and understandings that change depending on the data and technologies used, and the arguments emphasised, deep mapping resists a singular definition and a singular methodology. Aware of this, Bodenhamer asserts that at their heart

---

[64] Travis, 'GIS and History', p.182.   [65] Bodenhamer, Corrigan, and Harris, 'Preface', p.xiv.
[66] Bodenhamer, 'The Varieties of Deep Maps', p.5.
[67] Bauch, 'Designing for Mysterious Encounter', pp.39–45.
[68] Humphris, Horlings, and Biggs, 'Getting Deep into Things', p.12.
[69] www.cliffordmclucas.info/deep-mapping.html.

deep maps are simply new curated and creative spaces, and that deep maps defy clean definition as there are many types of deep map.[70]

The deep map at the heart of this Element is a literary map, and as such it draws and builds on the fields of literature and literary geography in its conceptualisation of deep mapping. One of the first to consider the potential of a literary deep map was Shelley Fisher Fishkin and she argues that literary deep maps are 'palimpsests in that they allow multiple versions of events, of texts, of phenomena to be written over each other'.[71] This process involves creating an interactive map, as the form of the display is geospatial in that it links text to location. In that way, it posits some relationship between the text and the location it is mapped to. By mapping multiple texts to multiple locations, the texts layer up, one on top of another, creating 'textual depth' and producing something akin to a geospatially organised literary anthology. Like other approaches to deep mapping this may involve the use of GIS, but it could also be achieved using platforms like OMEKA, or as in the case of MACMORRIS, custom-build platforms that employ a combination of different components like React JS, Mapbox, and deck.gl.

However, creating an interactive literary palimpsest is only one component of a literary deep map. Fisher Fishkin also advocates for four additional features to be included on the interactive displays for *literary* maps to be considered *deep* maps: (1) embed 'links to archival texts and images in nodes on an interactive map', (2) 'include links to texts and images in different locations', (3) incorporate multiple languages, (4) be open-access and be available as a pedagogical tool.[72] It is these extra components that make a literary map 'deep' as it is these features that truly ensure flexibility, immersion, exploration, and user-centred experiences. The literary deep map at the heart of this Element combines texts in a way that generates a palimpsest of literary culture in early modern Ireland and, specifically, our case study, the province of Munster. Equally, it incorporates the three key features that Fisher Fishkin proposes: it is open access and it ensures that users are brought to a digital version of the text being mapped where possible. However, the scope and impetus for the MACMORRIS deep map differ from the brief that Fisher Fishkin recommends, as each individual deep map takes a different approach to literary studies. While Fisher Fishkin advocates for using deep maps to facilitate a more transnational approach to American Literature, the MACMORRIS deep map and this Element instead argue that the combination of counter-mapping and deep mapping techniques

---

[70] Bodenhamer, 'The Varieties of Deep Maps', p.7. [71] Fisher Fishkin, 'Deep Maps', 3.
[72] Fisher Fishkin, 'Deep Maps', 2–3.

can produce decolonial strategies that can reimagine and enlarge what gets incorporated, and more importantly who/what gets read.

2.2 Decolonial Strategies for Literary Deep Mapping

> Decolonization, which sets out to change the order of the world, is, obviously, a program of complete disorder. But it cannot come as a result of magical practices, nor of a natural shock, nor of a friendly understanding. Decolonization, as we know, is a historical process: that is to say it cannot be understood, it cannot become intelligible nor clear to itself except in the exact measure that we can discern the movements which give it historical form and content.
>
> – *Franz Fanon, The Wretched of the Earth*[73]

A decolonial strategy for deep mapping uses the innate flexibility of a deep map to allow incompatible narratives to sit alongside one another, to give a platform to plurality without privileging any one viewpoint. Decoloniality is a critical theory that, at its starting point, assumes that history is not linear but that, instead, 'there are several histories, all simultaneous histories, inter-connected by imperial and colonial powers, by imperial and colonial differences'.[74] Through the act of drawing on and presenting these simultaneous histories, a decolonial deep map provides a platform where the 'program of complete disorder' that Fanon recommends can play out. On the deep map, 'disorder' registers as juxtaposition. Juxtaposition – the coincidence in the same space of discordant texts from multiple language traditions rubbing up against one another – produces the controlled 'disorder' of that often violent clash of viewpoints. In that way, it creates a pluriversal space. Decolonial deep mapping, then, is a 'politicized, passionate, and partisan' approach that uses digital maps to 'deconstruct the idea of a "post" colonial' and to 'make visible the cracks in universals while simultaneously opening up pluriversal spaces'.[75] It is a form of counter-mapping in that it 'mixes theory and practice to be productive and generative, a way to open, explore, and realize alternatives to the status quo'. Like counter-maps, decolonial deep maps are 'a methodological approach that unsettles and unpacks the spatial assumptions upon which maps are crafted and that troubles the spatial and temporal fixes of a state-based gaze', making it possible 'to re-evaluate the contribution of knowledge produced in colonial contexts'.[76] Like counter-maps, decolonial deep maps are one way in which the process of decolonisation can occur in practise, evident not only on the MACMORRIS deep map but in the counter-mapping endeavours of CMAP,

---

[73] Fanon, *The Wretched of the Earth*, p.36.   [74] Mignolo, 'Introduction', 155–56.
[75] www.cliffordmclucas.info/deep-mapping.html; Naylor et al., 'Interventions', 199–200.
[76] Boatcă, 'Counter-Mapping as Method', 245.

Decolonial Deep Mapping

as well as the Counter Cartographies Collective (3Cs), the Palestinian Counter-Cartography on Google Earth, and digital counter-mapping of Turtle Island.[77]

However, while all decolonial deep maps are counter-maps, not all counter-maps need to be deep maps. In fact, Craig Dalton and Tim Stallman argue that 'sometimes the best [counter]-map is no map at all'.[78] The difference between a counter-map and a decolonial deep map is not the use of GIS or equivalent platforms to present a map that challenges coloniality but the addition of interactive features and user-centred experience that enable an individual to engage with pluriversality. In this sense, decolonial deep maps offer a way of exploring the challenges of writing a decolonial history and of providing insights into otherwise repressed or forgotten pasts. Through its combination of texts, manuscript and map images drawn from a colonial context where coloniser and colonised actively confronted one another, a decolonial deep map is a digital 'third space'. This space is not the space of the coloniser, nor the 'before' space of the colonised. Neither is it the 'then' space of colonisation nor the 'now' space of coloniality. It is a third space where all of the complexities surrounding coloniser/colonised and then/now can get worked through. As decolonial deep maps do not synthesise textual selections into one overarching argument, they refuse to present one single answer. Instead, decolonial deep maps allow users to create their own permutations each time. This gives readers agency, by encouraging them to explore the additional features (including hyperlinked sources) for themselves.

Multiperspectivity and pluriversality, like decolonisation, are processes and strategies of understanding in which multiple perspectives are presented.[79] Both build from an understanding that historical narrative is constrained by the range of sources available, or selected. Multiperspectivity and pluriversality require – and are achieved by – an active kind of reading that extends – and challenges – the scope of historical accounts, by interrogating how different perspectives relate to each other and how they have been shaped by each other. This requires that groups marginalised in dominant historiographies are brought into these conversations.[80] Once restored, that additional dimension unsettles linear historiography by introducing a sequence of 'meanwhiles', or thinking 'otherwise', which deconstructs the colonial 'master' narrative by moving 'towards a fragmented, plural project'.[81] It makes apparent the multi-faceted nature of the

---

[77] Quiquivix, 'Art of War, Art of Resistance', 444–59; Dalton and Mason-Deese, 'Counter (Mapping) Actions', 439–66; Hunt and Stevenson, 'Decolonizing Geographies of Power', 372–92.
[78] Dalton and Stallman, 'Counter-mapping', 97.
[79] Fritzsche, 'Unable to Be Tolerant?' pp.1–9.
[80] Stradling, *Multiperspectivity in History Teaching*, p.19.
[81] Mignolo, 'Local Histories/Global Designs', 11.

past and shows how no single narrative reflects the whole story. It brings to the fore 'manifold local histories' and recovers the complexity of the original encounter by demonstrating that what colonists project as 'universal' history is nothing more than their own 'local history'.[82]

Decolonial deep mapping, then, is an important methodology for decolonial approaches to digital humanities. It responds to Roopika Risam's call for digital humanities to re-centre 'that which has traditionally been relegated to the position of subaltern in dominant narratives', as well as 'remediat[ing] colonial violence, writ[ing] back to colonial histories, and fill[ing] gaps in knowledge that remain a legacy of colonialism'.[83] Risam argues that digital approaches should engage in 'an exercise in world making', and since the development of deep maps involves negotiations about what is represented and how, they are a useful digital technique for facilitating a form of world making that offers perspectives 'exterior' (in Escobar's terms) to coloniality and, in doing so, recovers once-discarded but now once-again relevant imaginative resources for reconstructing the present.[84] The MACMORRIS deep map, to which we now turn, is a decolonial deep map as it engages in an act of decolonial requital, designed to recover a complexity and plurality – cultural, linguistic, political, ecological – rubbed out by colonial mapping and the territorial acquisition and redistribution it enabled.

The MACMORRIS deep map tests the potential of decolonial deep mapping to reassemble a lost linguistic plurality. It counters the dominant colonial narrative by presenting the Gaelic voices and perspectives erased by colonisation alongside it. In doing so, it responds to a long-standing blindspot in the way a crucial moment in the history of Ireland and Britain – the conquest of Ireland – has been understood. One of the consequences of the conquest was that English became the language of power, administration, and record; Irish became marginalised in key domains. The ongoing reproduction, by a largely anglophone scholarship, of that unbalanced archive means that early modern Ireland continues to be viewed through the writings of those most hostile to – and least knowledgeable about – Ireland. The deep map is fundamental to MACMORRIS's commitment to representing the viewpoint of the native Irish (and their continental allies), as well as the English. It provides a key visualisation for capturing the heterogenous, incompatible, and discordant narratives that emerge in a time (and place) of conquest and colonisation. It responds to the spatial logic of planters and natives living cheek-by-jowl, represented so graphically in Frances Jobson's map of the Munster Plantation in the previous section (see Figure 5). That real-world

---

[82] Escobar, 'Worlds and Knowledges Otherwise', 189.
[83] Risam, *New Digital Worlds*, p.45; Kirschenbaum, 'Hello Worlds'.
[84] Risam, *New Digital Worlds*, p.32.

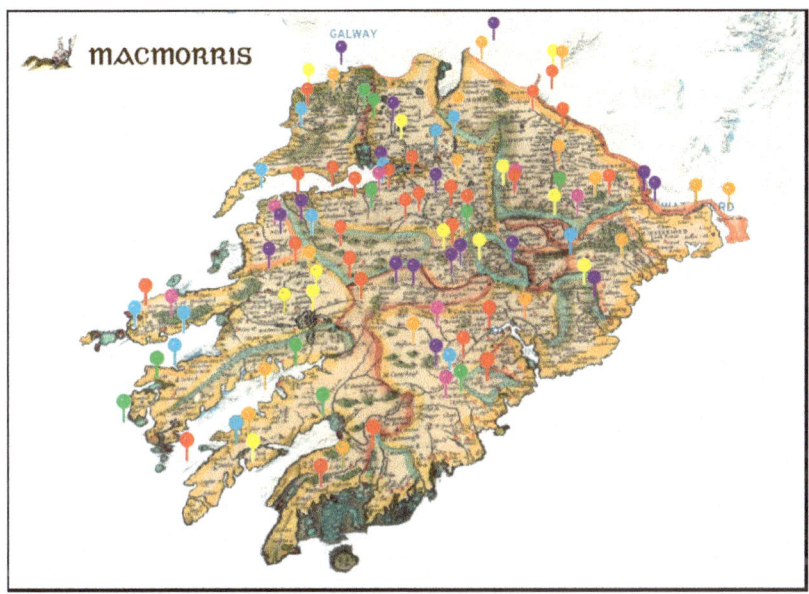

Figure 5 Deep map of Munster (www.macmorris.maynoothuniversity.ie/map) (Historical map layer courtesy of Trinity College Dublin).

contiguity of actors inhabiting very different cultural and ideological spaces meant the difference was already spatialised: planter poet already lived contiguous with Old English patron and Gaelic *file* (poet). By laying such incommensurable perspectives side by side, without privileging any one of them, the deep map reassembles complexity. The logic of a purely spatial arrangement – this English writer pops up alongside that Italian captain simply because they were in the same place at one time – flattens hierarchies in a way that challenges the notion that any one speaker (or anyone culture or language) has access to a universal truth.

2.3 The MACMORRIS Deep Map

The MACMORRIS deep map presents a literary map of Munster curated through a decolonial lens by putting the deep mapping techniques discussed in the previous two sections into practice. It presents a spatially ordered digital anthology of curated extracts that offers its users the raw materials for an open-ended exploration of the period's complexity. Its interface incorporates texts, illustrations, and digital map layers to generate the kind of interactive literary palimpsest advocated by Fisher Fishkin. Its literary depth comes not only from the wide array of texts presented side by side in their original language but also by enabling the reader to follow hyperlinks from the map to textual snippet, and then from the expanded extract to the full text. Overall, the texts selected come from a variety of genres and languages. They capture a dizzying range of forms, from hieratic eulogy to reports from a massacre, from Chancery writs to the keen observation of a natural historian, from a neo-Latin epic celebrating a Tipperary hero to an intelligence report on an elopement; it ranges from love poetry, divine and secular, to Spanish *relaciones* and plantation surveys. The textual and manuscript selections pay particular attention to bringing neglected Irish-language material back into the conversation. Subject specialists in Classical Irish and early modern English made their choices on the basis of the extracts' interest, quality, and representativeness, though there is no escaping the subjectivity inherent in any selection process. After all, deep maps are 'curated products'. They strive not for 'objectivity or authority but rather a negotiated conversation'.[85]

These selections are organised into seven different categories, each identified with its own coloured map-pin. These icon layers are as follows: lordship and patronage; cultural production; strategic or symbolic; conflict; performance, including music; the natural world (green); and a maritime, riverine (blue) layer. Those categories allow users to navigate the MACMORRIS deep map by following distinct thematic clusters. In total, 101 of the 207 extracts are in English (49%), 80 are in Irish (39%), 11 are in Spanish (5.3%), 10 are in Latin (5%), 4 are in Italian, and 1 is in German. Each of those 207 texts is allocated its particular place on the map, either because that is the place mentioned in the extract or it is a place associated with the writer or his or her subject. Each of the 101 places featured on the deep map is indicated by a map pin that, when clicked on, opens a window which presents between one and thirteen texts associated with that place. The MACMORRIS website as a whole is bilingual – a switcher allows users to move between Irish and English versions – so, in keeping with that policy, each placename is given in both English and Irish. Given the multiplicity of locales, texts, and languages, and the fact that any given place may host a variety of different texts on discrepant themes, a site of cultural production or lordship can simultaneously be – or can become – a strategic site or a place of violence. There is a similarly broad range within each category. One blue pin may bring us to a bardic account of swimming in the River Feale and walking amid the spindrift of 'gach trágha torcharaigh', 'each fruitful strand'; a second may bring us to a barque laden with biscuits and wine being lured onto a sandbank and ransacked.[86]

The presentation of these texts responds to the multilingualism of the texts themselves. On the map interface, the user only has access to the snippet view

---

[85] Bodenhamer, Corrigan, and Harris, eds. 'Introduction', p.21.
[86] www.macmorris.maynoothuniversity.ie/site/102; www.macmorris.maynoothuniversity.ie/site/120.

rather than the full textual extract. The user can go from location to location and explore the snippets mapped on the various locations (see Figure 6). Or they can read more by opening a new tab and, indeed, keep multiple tabs open in order to compare the different texts and their various perspectives. The map is designed to work in this way rather than allowing multiple pop ups and multiple texts to be set against each other on one screen, for both practical and argumentative purposes. In terms of practicalities, the 207 extracts amount to over 40,000 words with some extracts coming in at over 500 words. To allow multiple extended passages to pop up on the map interface itself would crowd out the screen and be difficult to navigate, hindering 'deep' engagement. This in turn would detract from the overall aim of encouraging close reading of an expanded corpus. More importantly, however, we felt that the map interface should only include the original language of the text so that users cannot override the fact that the complex story of early modern Ireland was being told in several languages, and not just English. Thus, users must engage with the multilingual reality of the region. By tabbing out rather than popping, or layering, up, we give the original language priority on the map itself, while also allowing the new tab to present the text alongside a parallel translation (when the text is from a non-anglophone source). This facilitates a more user-friendly access to the sources. The parallel translations allow for a deeper reading of the full range of extracts, enabling users, irrespective of their language competencies, to pick their way through the decolonialised corpus and form their own palimpsests from the texts available through the deep map (see Figure 7).

Another important element of the map interface is the image illustrating the pop-up window for each location on the map. The images, drawn from contemporary manuscripts and colonial maps, add a visual dimension for each place. The manuscript images of Irish texts give a sense of the materiality of Gaelic cultural production, as well as conveying the vibrancy of Gaelic script. These include samples of bardic poetry, a legal text, and an extract from the *Annals of the Four Masters*.[87] A detail from a contemporary map may offer a cartographic snapshot of a given location, or it may be extracted from one of the drawings embellishing those maps, such as the crude sketch of 'Desmond beheaded', placed at Glanageenty (Gleann na Ginte), where the 15th Earl of Desmond was hacked to death (see Figure 8).[88]

---

[87] Manuscript images of bardic poetry is available at Nohavaldaly (Nuachabháil Uí Dhálaigh), Thurles (Dúrlas), Shanid (Seanaid), and Askeaton (Eas Géitine). The image of a Gaelic legal text is mapped to Ballymacegan (Baile Mhic Aogáin), while the *Annals of the Four Masters* is mapped to Derrinlaur (Doire an Láir).

[88] The drawing of 'Desmond Beheaded' is from Speed, *The Invasions of England and Ireland with All Their Civill Wars since the Conquest*.

Figure 6 Deep map of Munster (www.macmorris.maynoothuniversity.ie/map) (Nohavaldaly | Nuachabháil Uí Dhálaigh and snippet view of Bean dá chumhadh críoch Ealla).

MACMORRIS

Home / Search the Database / Site

CITE THIS DATA

Quatrains to Aonghus Fionn Ó Dálaigh (1602)

Text

41 Ó Dálaigh an dréachta ghlóin, mac ochta chloinne Carthaigh, dalta an chróchshlóigh mhálla mhir, órthóir an dána dhírigh.

42 Bádhadh trúdha, tobar fis, cosg dubha, dúsgadh áinis, léaghadh meall nglanrolla ngeal, ceann foghloma na bhfilleadh.

43 Ursa breithnighthe gréas ngill, sgolaidhe d'ollamh inghill, altra cháigh i n-ar gceird-ne, fáidh glanta na Gaoidhelge.

I gcló/In print: Lambert McKenna, Dioghluim dána, Baile Átha Cliath (1938), poem 73.

Text

41 Ó Dálaigh of faultless poetry, a son of the bosom of Clann Carthaigh, fostering of the swift and gentle saffron host, gilder of Dán Díreach.

42 Suppressing [sntuí] desire, a well of knowledge, reproving darkness, awakening delight, studying masses of bright and faultless scrolls, the poets head of learning.

43 Pillar of adjudication for praiseworthy works of art, foster-father of everyone of our craft, scholars of an excellent master-poet, the polished prophet of the Irish language.

Aistriúchán/Translation: Philip Mac a' Ghoill

Alternative Title	Bean dá chumhadh críoch Ealla
Site Type	Cultural Production
Place	Nohavaldaly
Author	Fear Feasa Ón Cháinte
References	https://bardic.celt.dias.ie/displayPoem.php?firstL=z4&D=301
Connected People	Fear Feasa Ón Cháinte | Aonghus Ó Dálaigh Fionn

Figure 7 Deep map of Munster (https://macmorris.maynoothuniversity.ie/site/20) (Quatrains to Aonghus Fionn Ó Dálaigh (1602).

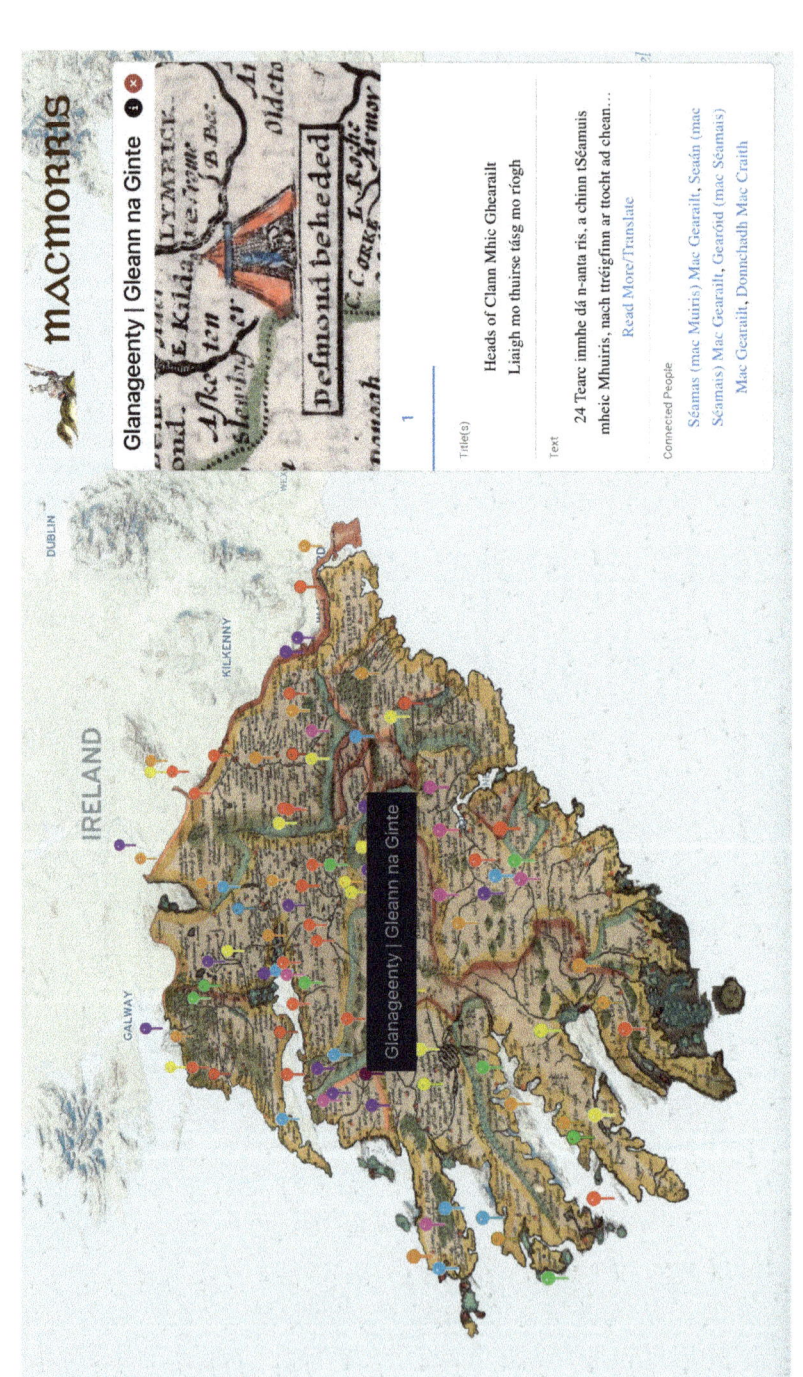

Figure 8 Deep map of Munster (www.macmorris.maynoothuniversity.ie/map) (Glanageenty | Gleann na Ginte and snippet view of Liaigh mo thuirse tásg mo ríogh).

In each instance the illustration adds depth either by providing a visual context for the texts represented at any given location or by implicitly challenging the historical map layer, by highlighting the features emphasised and omitted.[89] For Glanageenty the image provides visual context: the crude sketch is accompanied by a Gaelic poem in which the poet Donnchadh Mac Craith mourns the loss of his patron and grieves at the fact that Desmond's head was brought 'soir ó Shliabh Luachra go Lunndoin', 'east from Sliabh Luachra to London'. In other instances, like Nohavaldaly (Nuachabháil Uí Dhálaigh), the illustration challenges the historical map's representation. The map's depiction of a blank space is syncopated with evidence that this area was, in reality, home to the bardic school that produced that striking Gaelic script.

The MACMORRIS deep map in its totality is an experiment in creating a visualisation that enables new ways of seeing by putting the elements in place for going beyond the colonial perspective. The juxtaposition of disparate texts and images, which are connected only by the coincidence of the space in which they were written or which they write about, doesn't just show us the contours of incommensurate world views. It brings back into circulation the full range of perspectives that marked the original encounter, including, crucially, those that would, as a consequence of colonisation, fall (or be pushed) out of history. Robertson and Mullen argue that the multiplicity that characterises deep maps must 'enable multiple meanings to be made by its users'.[90] The deep map offers a corrective to dominant monolingual historiographies by presenting the multivalent, multilingual, and multiperspective voices of the past in a non-hierarchical and non-linear way. By challenging historians and literary scholars writing from our current moment of coloniality to engage with that full range of material, we encourage them, too, to reflect on the continuum between colonisation and coloniality. This continuum chimes with another pluriversality at play in the deep map and adding to its 'depth' – pluriversal temporalities.

2.4 Decolonising through Pluriversal Temporalities

The first and most explicit temporality is the past, the events and multiple perspectives narrated by the sources. This temporality is the heart of the deep map. It is through this temporality that users engage in multilingual comparative readings, in order to understand the views, perspectives, and beliefs of the different historical agents, including those whose perceptions were sidelined. The temporal zone of the deep map represents the 'then' of colonisation and the emergence of a settler colonial society in Ireland. Eve Tuck and K. Wayne Yang

---

[89] Harley, *History of Cartography. Vol. 1.*
[90] Robertson and Mullen, 'Navigating through Narrative', p.133.

argue that 'everything within a settler colonial society strains to destroy or assimilate the Native in order to disappear them from the land'.[91] In Ireland, this process occurred over the sixteenth and seventeenth centuries, and to engage with the textual material on the deep map linearly – and, by implication, teleologically – would simply restate the settler colonial narrative of Gaelic defeat and English victory. However, despite spanning thirty-eight years, there is no temporal sequencing on the deep map. Here, everything is happening all at once and no one event has temporal priority. Instead, the entire span is condensed into a 'then' time encompassing both conquest and that which stood to be conquered. This ensures that the extracts are detached from teleology ('the end of Gaelic Ireland'). Thus, by moving around the deep map and engaging with sources from the early 1570s on the same spatial plane as the late 1590s, the user is forced to choose between trying to re-impose chronology and engaging with the past as one messy temporality where no one universal truth dominates. By deconstructing teleology, the deep map opens up a space where subaltern perspectives and forms of knowledge live once again, in the deep map's historical present.[92]

The second temporal layer is the gap between the past and the present – a historiographical layer that is made up of the perspectives of those who have created narratives of a particular historical event and its interpretation.[93] It is in this temporal layer that 'coloniality' becomes embedded and versions of the past are constructed for present consumption. None of these historiographical and literary interpretations are explicitly represented on the deep map but, as their interpretations have been absorbed into the public memory and academic research, the deep map is inevitably in conversation with them. Sometimes this is a conscious conversation, as is the case with the provocative placement of Edmund Spenser's dedicatory sonnet to Arthur Grey at Smerwick which brings together the often artificially separated domains of 'literature' and 'history' and, here, patronage and massacre.[94] Sometimes it is less deliberate in that the deep map contains texts that have also been used by previous generations of scholars.

---

[91] Tuck and Yang, 'Decolonisation Is Not a Metaphor', 9.
[92] For more on this concept see Mignolo, 'Local Histories/Global Designs', 9–11.
[93] For a good explanation of this temporal layer and how it relates to other temporal layers see Wansink et al. 'Where Does Teaching Multiperspectivity in History Education Begin and End?' 499.
[94] The Smerwick Massacre was a crunch episode of the Second Desmond War, 1579–1583, in which a papal force of around 600 Spanish and Italian landed at Smerwick and began to fortify Dún an Óir, a prehistoric fort. On 7 November 1580, Lord Deputy Arthur Grey, alongside his secretary (Edmund Spenser) and 800 soldiers (including Walter Raleigh), bombarded the fort. After two days of continuous fire, the papal forces sought to surrender but after the papal officers marched out of the fort to surrender, Grey ordered that Raleigh alongside Humphrey Mackworth execute the 600 prisoners in the fort, which they did, disposing of the bodies by throwing them over the cliff. See Carey, 'Atrocity and History', pp.83–84.

The deep map is in implicit conversation with this historiographical temporal layer when it represents texts that have not been used as frequently as a basis for interpretation, or when it engages with concepts that have often been downplayed by historiography, such as violence.[95]

The third temporal layer is the most difficult to define, but arguably the most important to the processes of decolonial deep mapping. This is the present (or future presents), that is, the moment in which a user engages with the deep map. This temporal layer is the 'now' of modernity/coloniality. It is in this temporal layer that everything gets worked through, when users, implicitly or explicitly, participate in the untidy process of reconciliation or decolonisation, drawing together their own understanding of the two other temporal layers. In this temporal moment, they are confronted with the multilingual – multiversal – reality of the sources, and since the textual selections are not resolved into one master narrative, they must engage in processes that require them to pay greater attention to non-anglophone sources. That involves grappling with how the various communities perceived each other's actions and motives, and relating that to what they already know about the historical moment under consideration – all processes that are important steps towards a decolonial history. Margeret Marietta Ramírez argues that 'decolonization must mean attending to ghosts, and arresting widespread denial of the violence done to them.' Thus, users in the 'now' of coloniality must choose how they want to attend to the ghosts of the 'then' and engage in their own 'politics of decolonial accountability'.[96]

Bringing these three temporalities together constitutes a decolonial praxis. This praxis 'requires re-embodiment, interrogating one's relationship to colonialism'.[97] In the case of the MACMORRIS deep map, this praxis involves the act of reading *with* the grain of the deep map, rather than following the postcolonial practice of reading *against* the grain of colonial texts. In *Culture and Imperialism*, Edward Said argues that canonical colonial texts should be read contrapuntally, in that readings of such texts should 'draw out, extend, give emphasis and voice to what is

---

[95] For most of the twentieth century Irish historians had little to say about the violence that characterised early modern Ireland. Clodagh Tait, David Edwards, and Pádraig Lenihan point the finger at T.W. Moody, D.B Quinn, and R. Dudley Edwards, and the revisionist tendencies of this era, noting that from the formation of *Irish Historical Studies* in 1938 until 1989 no articles were published that grappled fully with violence. However, the 1990s heralded a change as it coincided with a resurgence in interest in the early modern period and the production, due to theoretical and methodological advances, of a wider array of histories and approaches, including social, cultural, economic, gender, literary, and local histories. For more on this see Tait, Edwards, and Lenihan, 'Early Modern Ireland', pp.14–15; Bradshaw, 'And so Began the Irish Nation'; Bradshaw, 'Nationalism and Historical Scholarship in Modern Ireland', 329–51. There are also recent conversation on what it means to decolonise Irish history. See Nic Dháibhéid et al. 'Round Table', pp.303–32.

[96] Naylor et al., 'Interventions', 204–206.   [97] Naylor et al., 'Interventions', 206.

silent or marginally present', in a way that takes accounts of both imperialism and resistance.[98] This has become the cornerstone of a postcolonial approach to literature leading to important scholarship that pinpointed the colonial inflection of several texts on the MACMORRIS deep map.[99] However, to read canonical texts contrapuntally and not stray beyond them means to remain within the confines of canonical coloniality. (As Ropika Risam observes, all too often, Digital Humanities means 'the digital canonical humanities'.)[100] To read *with* the grain of the deep map, however, is to supplement Said's contrapuntal reading with a reading practise that goes beyond the colonial canon and juxtaposes colonial texts with marginalised, non-anglophone texts. This type of reading allows users to craft their own engagement with multiplicity and pluriversality. Moreover, it does so in a way that presents all the contending viewpoints as culturally equal, potentially bringing each user towards new insights and opening up new decolonial possibilities. In short, juxtaposition functions as a way of introducing the 'disorder' which Fanon identified as central to the praxis of decolonisation, on a textual dimension. Because juxtaposition is a key factor of our reading strategy and because we see it as a necessary supplement to Said's practice of 'contrapuntal' reading, we call our reading strategy 'juxtapuntal'.

Of course, as users navigate their own way through the deep map, it is possible for them to read against the grain of the deep map, by engaging, say, with one set of perspectives while ignoring others. Users could, wilfully, try to reinscribe the hierarchies and silos that the deep map breaks down. But in the act of engaging with material in this way, the user would be forced to confront their own reasons for bypassing alternative perspectives, which is itself still a step – an early step, perhaps – in that user's own non-linear process of decolonisation. But, to enable as many users as possible to go with the grain of the MACMORRIS deep map, we turn next to consider what we mean by juxtapuntal reading.

3 Decolonial Reading Strategies: Archives, Contiguity, and the Juxtapuntal

Early modern Ireland, we are told, was a barbarous place. Those who tell us that were those who coveted it – those who invaded it, conquered it with pitiless violence, and colonised it. Anthony Nixon's 'England's Hope against Ireland's

---

[98] Said, *Culture and Imperialism*, pp.66–67.
[99] Examples of this include the numerous important studies relating to Edmund Spenser. See Maley, *Salvaging Spenser*; Herron, *Spenser's Irish Work*; Coughlan, *Spenser and Ireland*; Burlinson, *Allegory, Space, and the Material World in the Writings of Edmund Spenser*; Hadfield, *Spenser's Irish Experience*.
[100] Risam, *New Digital Worlds*, p.16.

Hate' (c. 1600) reads like a bricolage of all the glib tropes: the Irish are 'wod borne Savages... dunghill gnats', and 'rebellious Swine' whose 'snowtes' need '[r]inging'.[101] With little beyond a papal bull (Adrian IV's *Laudabiliter* of 1155) to back their claims, and frustrated by the resistance of an enemy whom they were programmed to underestimate, the Tudor agents of conquest resorted to denigration to justify their actions. Their engagement with Gaelic culture and the Irish language rarely extended beyond execrating both. It is paradoxical, therefore, that these very texts remain the principal – and very often the only – conduit through which historians and literary scholars approach early modern Ireland. But, no matter how hard such texts are read 'against the grain', or in Said's terms 'contrapuntally', they cannot give us access to a Gaelic world to which they themselves had no *entrée*. This problematic afterlife of colonial discourse produces a double silencing familiar to the colonised everywhere: those who were silenced in the past are silenced again when their culture is reconstructed from the writings of those who had the power to project their own ignorance as knowledge. MACMORRIS models a way of putting those whom colonialism pushed off the map back onto it. It then offers a practice, which we call juxtapuntal reading, that allows subalternised texts and perspectives to challenge and disrupt interpretations made hegemonic by colonialism. In doing so, MACMORRIS offers a template for those working in other decolonising contexts where – and this is not always the case – alternative archives exist.

3.1 Moving beyond the Colonial Archive

A reliance on anglophone sources is itself a product of the twin legacies of colonisation – on the one hand, the destruction of native learning and the violent abrogation of its right to a future and, on the other, linguistic colonisation. After all, the present hegemony of English is itself an outgrowth of a process set in motion in sixteenth-century Ireland: English, then just another jobbing national vernacular, hemmed in by other languages even on its own island, takes its first step towards global dominance, in what Friedrich Engels called 'England's first colony'.[102] One of the few consistent threads in Tudor policy was its hostility to Irish and its promotion of English. The 1537 'Act for the English Order, Habite, and Language', for example, required 'all men that will knowledge themselves to be his Highness true and faithfull subjects' to use 'the said English tongue'.[103] As native lords surrendered, the terms of their pardons required

---

[101] Carpenter, *Verse in English from Tudor and Stuart Ireland*, pp.98–107, pp.105–106; an extract can be found at site 52, Askeaton.
[102] Marx and Engels, *Marx and Engels on Ireland*, p.83.
[103] *The Statutes at Large Passed in the Parliaments held in Ireland*, pp.120–21.

them to 'bring up their children ... in the use of the English tongue'.[104] But legislation, policy, and prohibitions targeting professional poets could only go so far.[105] Defeat and exile did the rest. After the rout at Kinsale (1601) and the 'Flight of the Earls' (1607), the schools of poetry, history, law, and medicine where the learned class or *aos ealadhan* learned their craft confronted both the collapse of patronage and a new order that had no place for their knowledge. English became the language of administration, law, education, and commerce. The decline of Irish as a language of power had begun; meanwhile, English was in expansionist mode.

But, at the time of the conquest, 'the great silence' lay far in the future.[106] It is imperative, therefore, that we don't narrate this – or any other – site of early modern rupture as though the silence had already happened. The disequilibrium that characterises modern scholarship did not exist in early modern Ireland. Certainly, English brought the energies of the Elizabethan Renaissance along on its expansionist journey. But Irish, with a constantly regenerating literary tradition reaching back to at least the sixth century, was also at the top of its game. What Amardeep Singh calls 'the Archive Gap' simply does not exist for early modern Ireland.[107] There are 1107 bardic poems alone in the MACMORRIS 'works' database; hyperlinks bring us to the text of every one of these poems of counsel, praise, and power-brokerage.[108] The methodological challenge of reinserting a rich if grievously underutilised archive into a hitherto one-sided conversation is a luxury compared to the problem usually facing decolonial scholars – the absence of any countervailing archive. Saidiya Hartman highlights – and offers a way through – the challenge of telling an 'impossible story', a story where none of the available sources were written by its subalternised protagonists. How, Hartman asks, do we tell the story of African women caught up in the violence of the Atlantic slave trade, when the only glimpses of their lives and deaths come from the records of their tormentors, from 'the fictions of history ... and [the] fantasies that constitute the archive'? Hartman reaches for 'critical fabulation' as a strategy for moving beyond the gaps and lies in the archive and supplying that deficit imaginatively.[109] Margaret Pearce and Michael Hermann's decolonising map of Samuel de Champlain's seventeenth-century travels among the Anishinabec,

---

[104] Morrin, ed. *Calendar of the Patent and Close Rolls of Chancery of Ireland*, vol. 1, p.81.
[105] Palmer, *Language and Conquest in Early Modern Ireland*, p.138.
[106] On that – later – language shift, see de Fréine, *The Great Silence*; McCloskey, *Voices Silenced: Has Irish a Future? / Guthanna in Éag: An Mairfidh an Ghaeilge Beo?*; Slomanson, 'On the Great Silence', 95–114.
[107] Singh, 'Beyond the Archive Gap', 237–51.
[108] www.macmorris.maynoothuniversity.ie/network.
[109] Hartman, 'Venus in Two Acts', 1–14, 9, 11.

Wendat, Wabanaki, and Innu responds to the silence of the archive by imaginatively reconstructing native voices. Their narrative map brings 'Native and non-Native geographies and journals together ... using narrative technique to encode for place, to subvert the conventions of historical cartography, and address the colonial silences and emotional emptiness of that practice'. In the absence of any surviving indigenous testimonies, they can create a 'place ... defined by multiple voices' only by setting '*imagined* native voices' alongside 'Champlain's voice ... quoted directly from his journals (typeset in blue)'.[110] When seeking to decolonise our understanding of early modern Ireland, in contrast, there is no need to imagine the native voice, no 'straining against the limits of the archive';[111] there is simply the obligation to open the archive – and *read*.

Except, of course, it isn't that simple. Even those committed to writing more inclusive histories of conquest and colonisation struggle to make the leap. Gaelic records may be extensive but they are nothing as accessible as the English archive; swathes of bardic poetry, for example, remain unedited, untranslated, and largely out of reach of those without Classical Irish.[112] But the imbalance which the MACMORRIS project confronted is not just a consequence of the contrasting fates of the Irish and English languages. Even more fundamentally, it arises from one of colonialism's foundational strategies, the 'subalternization of the knowledge and cultures' of the colonised.[113] Bernard Cohn's discussion of what he calls 'forms of knowledge' helps to explain the process. In premodern states, he suggests, '[t]he theatre of power was managed by specialists (priests and ritual preceptors, historians and bards, artists and artisans) who maintained the various forms of knowledge required'. Colonisation, however, entailed the conquest not only of territory but of 'epistemological space'.[114] This epistemological conquest involved both the marginalisation of native knowledge and the valorisation of a new, empirical way of knowing the world. New English colonists deprecated indigenous Irish knowledge at every turn, condemning it as the work of 'blindly and brutishly informed' natives. Spenser, whose insult that is, is representative in dismissing Irish forms of knowledge: 'Irish Chronicles ... are most fabulous and forged',

---

[110] Pearce and Hermann, 'Decolonizing Historical Cartography through Narrative', quoted in Wood, *Power of Maps*, 133–34 (our emphasis), and '"They Would Not Take Me There": People, Places, and Stories from Champlain's Travels in Canada, 1603–1616': www.umaine.edu/canam/publications/champlain-mapthey-would-not-take-me-there/– Description.

[111] Hartman, 'Venus in Two Acts', 11.

[112] The scale of the task is exemplified by McManus and Ó Raghallaigh eds., *A Bardic Miscellany*, which transcribes and provides diplomatic editions (but no translations) for 500 poems 'which richly deserve ... complete editions', p.xxxi.

[113] Escobar, 'Worlds and Knowledges Otherwise', 184.

[114] Cohn, *Colonialism and Its Forms of Knowledge*, pp.3, 4.

he declared, insisting that Irish historians merely concoct 'Milesian lyes', and that Irish poets 'forge and falsifie every thing as they list'.[115] In contrast, the English vaunted their purchase on 'facts'. Sir Francis Bacon's briefing on Irish affairs for the Earl of Essex, for example, proposes a scientific method for fact-finding:

> if a resolution be taken, a consultation must proceed; and the consultation must be governed upon information to be had from such as know the place, and matters in fact; and in taking of information I have always noted there is a skill and a wisdom.[116]

Cohn traces the emergence of colonial 'forms of knowledge' with its empirical regime of facts to British imperial activity in eighteenth-century India. But, in keeping with Escobar insistence that modernity/coloniality emerges in early modernity rather than, say, the Enlightenment, we can see that the epistemological breach was already opening up, two centuries earlier, in Ireland (among other places).[117]

Clearly then, authoritative 'forms of knowledge', to use Cohn's term, were already being elevated over forms deemed specious – forged, fabulous, and false – in early modern Ireland. This factitious but convenient dichotomy – the colonists had access to truth, while the colonised had only 'lies' – gets to the heart of why we needed to make the MACMORRIS deep map. If we are to decolonise the anglophone literary canon relating to Ireland, we need to confront the epistemic shift towards scientific rationalism and empiricism which was used to marginalise native forms of knowledge in colonial contexts. After all, Spenser and Bacon's attempt to fix the boundaries of what is evidentially admissible – what can and cannot be credited – sits within a regime of knowledge that continues to privilege the colonial archive over the sources of the colonised. The evidential protocols of what E. H. Carr calls 'the commonsense view of history'[118] map perfectly onto forms of knowledge which would have met with Spenser and Bacon's approval. Sources like the (English) State Papers are recognisable as repositories of the 'so-called basic facts' (Carr again) in a way that bardic poems, say, are not.

The MACMORRIS project emerged, in large measure, in response to the damaging exclusion of Irish-language sources from accounts of early modern Ireland. For far too long, scholars of English literature attempted to conduct a 'dialogue' – itself a very questionable concept in the context of colonial

---

[115] Spenser, *View*, p.85, p.46, p.49.
[116] Hiram Morgan ed., *Sir Francis Bacon's MSS Relating to Ireland*, CELT: Corpus of Electronic Texts: www.celt.ucc.ie/published/E600001-015.html.
[117] Escobar, 'Worlds and Knowledges Otherwise', 184. [118] Carr, *What Is History?* p.8.

silencing – between Irish and English perspectives even as they restricted themselves exclusively to largely canonical – and often colonial – English texts. But of course, no early modern English-language text, no matter how contrapuntally it is read, can adequately represent the voice of 'the Other', much less articulate one side of a 'dialogue' properly conducted across cultures and languages.[119] For many historians, too, Gaelic sources tend to be treated as, at best, merely supplementary to the dominant archive. Some even go beyond ignoring or paying lip service to such sources. In his volume for Cambridge University Press's 'Critical Perspectives on Empire' series, for example, John Patrick Montaño asserts that Ireland was 'a predominantly oral culture' where even its laws were never written down, producing, he claims, 'a perfect example of Jacques Derrida's *mal d'archive*'. So, it remains entirely possible, even when ostensibly offering a 'critical perspectives on Empire', to offer a reading of early modern Ireland which draws exclusively on English colonial sources.[120]

This is slowly beginning to change. Digital resources, particularly the *Irish Bardic Poetry Database* and *Léamh*, have facilitated greater engagement with Gaelic material, by making available both Irish-language material *and* the linguistic, glossarial, and grammatical tools needed to use them.[121] The work of those using sources in Irish, Latin, and other languages, in addition to the English archive, is starting to rewrite our understanding of early modern Ireland.[122] The MACMORRIS deep map, therefore, might be seen as the cartographic wing of that endeavour. If cartography is one of the pre-eminently empirical practices of imperialism,[123] decolonial deep mapping offers a way of redrawing and countering the colonial map. It allows us to assemble a more inclusive miscellany of materials, linguistically, formally, and epistemologically. In diagnosing the real (as opposed to Montaño's imagined) '*mal d'archive*', Derrida begins by focusing on its location, its 'domiciliation' close to the centre of power. Archives occupy 'a privileged *topology*. They inhabit this unusual place, this place of election where law and singularity intersect in *privilege*'.[124] The very different – and literal – topology of the deep map offers a space where 'singularity' confronts plurality, and contention and dissent take the place of 'law' and 'election'.

---

[119] Palmer, 'Missing Bodies'.
[120] Montaño, *The Roots of English Colonialism in Ireland*, p.11; Brehon Law was, of course, written down.
[121] See the Irish Bardic Poetry Database, www.bardic.celt.dias.ie/, and Léamh, www.léamh.org.
[122] E.g. Harris ed., *Making Ireland Roman*; O'Connor, *Irish Voices from the Spanish Inquisition*; Kane and Wadden eds., *An Eoraip*.
[123] See, for example, Breen, 'The Empirical Eye', 44–52.
[124] Derrida, 'Archive Fever', 9–63, 10; Derrida's italics.

3.2 Contiguity, Assemblage, and Negotiating the Pluriverse Juxtapuntally

'A deep map is in many respects like a digital collection of primary sources', Robertson and Mullen tell us. But they worry that, in 'turn[ing] the task of authorship over to the user', deep maps run the risk of being little more than a collection of disaggregated texts. A deep map, in 'representing many perspectives[,] may have the effect of representing none of them', rendering the multiplicity it assembles 'mute in the midst of its chaos'. 'A deep map', they explain, 'invites the user of the map to craft his or her own experience through the multiplicity of sources made available'. But this is a fraught invitation: 'it appears that the audiences for humanities mapping do not necessarily want to explore a map to find an argument or construct a narrative, or are not equipped to do so.' Creators of deep maps, therefore, cannot simply 'let the past speak for itself, because it cannot. The aim of the deep map should be to translate for the past so that it can speak'. That is why deep mapping, like digital collecting more generally, they argue, is now 'facing a question about the place of argument or narrative. We are now at a point where we want more from mapping than a means of exploring sources'. For that reason, '[d]igital historians are facing calls for digital history to make arguments'.

'The act of creating a deep map', Robertson and Mullen insist, is always at least 'implicitly argumentative'.[125] The MACMORRIS deep map goes further: it is *explicitly* argumentative. It aims to 'challenge dominant anglophone (and, therefore, largely colonial) accounts of early modern Ireland', by layering complexity back in and, thereby, putting 'in place the resources for understanding what stood to be lost in a time of dynamic and often violent encounter'.[126] At one level, the argument lies in the selection process itself. It pushes back against the monovocality of colonialism – and its successor, coloniality – by placing subalternised texts on an equal footing with colonial ones. At another level, the argument comes from the assemblage of the deep map itself and the various 'assemblages' that make up the map. Our understanding of 'assemblage' is shaped by Gilles Deleuze and Felix Guattari, as well as Manuel Delanda, who argues that an 'assemblage' is a whole 'whose properties emerge from the interactions between parts'.[127] In Delanda's conception, an assemblage is comprised of parts that are contingent rather than necessary, and these parts can be taken out and used in other assemblages.[128] This is the case with the

---

[125] Robertson and Mullen, 'Navigating through Narrative', pp.132–35.
[126] https://macmorris.maynoothuniversity.ie/.
[127] Delanda, *A New Philosophy of Society*, p.5. See also Deleuze and Guattari, *A Thousand Plateaus*.
[128] Delanda, *A New Philosophy of Society*, p.9.

MACMORRIS deep map, which is made up – or is an assemblage – of texts, manuscript images, and map extracts, all brought together on an interactive geospatial digital interface – itself made up of an assemblage of code which draws on different coding libraries. As each part of the assemblage is contingent, each element of the deep map could be considered to be an assemblage in and of itself. When the textual selections are brought into a further assemblage with the geospatial interface, the sum of the different parts creates new, combinative meanings of place. This is because places are not fixed and stable; rather, they are states of continuous change.[129] Thus, when the textual selections interact with the places they are mapped to, they come together to form a part of the meaning of that place. By purposefully pluralising the meanings of different places throughout Munster, the assembled whole of the deep map makes explicit arguments about the linguistic and cultural plurality of the region at the height of the English conquest.

But the question remains: How do users craft their own individual negotiations with that material, ideally to decolonial affect? For Robertson and Mullen, the answer is to provide 'specific pathways through the map designed to tell a story'. 'Without a place to begin, and a pathway to follow, [users] spend little time engaging with digital maps.'[130] The 'pathway' metaphor and its conceptual cognates – journeys, starting- and end-points – are problematic, however, in a map vowed to resisting the inevitability of colonialism and to challenging coloniality's tendentious belief that 'there is/was no alternative'. Pathways are ontologically prior to the journey. They preexist those who travel along them. They presume a destination already foretold. They move, inexorably, along a teleological axis. Teleology, as we will see later, is precisely what this deep map seeks to resist. As Robertson and Mullen acknowledge, 'there is tension between the linearity inherent in the notion of a pathway and the ability to capture complexity that maps offer.'[131] MACMORRIS, therefore, eschews the 'pathway' path, opting instead for a more static – and yet, for colonial purposes, paradoxically more dynamic – cartographic effect: contiguity, or the sheer fact of alongsidedness. The rest of this section, accordingly, explores contiguity as the cartographic expression of colonial intrusion. Contiguity is the master trope of a troubled adjacency where the incommensurate world views of native and newcomer were held in equilibrium in a place and time of suspended outcomes. Contiguity is all about juxtaposition; the syncopations that emerge from those juxtapositions are central to we call 'juxtapuntal reading'.

---

[129] Dovey, *Becoming Places*, p.3.
[130] Robertson and Mullen, 'Navigating through Narrative', pp. 133, 134.
[131] Robertson and Mullen, 'Navigating through Narrative', p. 134.

3.3 Mapping the Contiguous Worlds of Coloniser and Colonised

In Section 1, we looked at Frances Jobson's 'Province of Munster' (TNA MPF 1/68), which provided a snapshot of the plantation in 1589. We return to it now because it is, so strikingly, a map of contiguity. It exemplifies to a remarkable degree the way in which colonial maps, for all their silences and omissions, let slip insights that exceed the instrumental purposes of their commissioning. Claims, practices, and understandings alien to the mapmaker's purpose still find a place on his map. While Jobson's focus is the plantation and its planters (men like Sir Walter Raleigh and Edmund Spenser), it cannot quite erase the cultural vibrancy and insistent native presence that continued to coexist alongside both. A bony finger of land pointing into the Atlantic is labelled simply 'RYMERS', acknowledging that Sheepshead Peninsula was home to two bardic schools. The names of Irish lords still in possession of their ancestral land are splayed in untidy capitals across mountain icons ('MACAR TE MOOR') or messily squeezed in between rivers and inlets ('C L A N M OR RISHE'), their territories 'distinguished the on[e] from the other wth severall colors'. Jobson explained to Burleigh that he had 'set downe' the plantation 'parcells', so that Elizabeth I's Chief Secretary could 'be holde' how the seignories of the undertakers 'but and bounde' with each other, and 'wth such other landes as are vnto them adiecent'. For this is a world of contiguity, where the newcomers, the dispossessed, and those still clinging to their land were indeed staggeringly 'adiecent'. This 'adjacency', this pattern of 'but[ting] and bound[ing]', is the key to the deep map's methodology. For what is 'adiecent' to the plantation seignories is nothing less than the immensity of a highly articulate Gaelic and Gaelicised world – a world utterly at odds with the centralising, expansionist, proto-capitalist, English Protestant reality that had landed in its midst.

The half-achieved conquest represented by the Munster Plantation is a world where Gaelic and Old English lords and intellectuals lived alongside the newcomers who sought to usurp them. The defeat of Hugh O'Neill's Confederates at the end of the Nine Years War – and the 'Flight of the Earls' (1607) which followed – brought that unstable cohabitation to an end. But for the thirty-eight years (1569– 1607) covered by the MACMORRIS deep map, two civilisations were still 'adjacent': native and newcomer 'butted and bounded' one another. Edmund Spenser's seignory was bounded to the east and west by the lordships of Roche and Barry, significant patrons of bardic poetry; their estates, in turn, were butted against from the south by Thomas Norris, Lord President of Munster, castle builder, and iron-ore prospector. At its eastern bounds, Herbert's seignory abutted the seat of the Earls of Desmond's hereditary poets; to the north, his estate was bounded by the powerful MacMorris lordship, a magnet for visiting poets, and, to the south, by the 26th Mac Carthaigh Mór, counterreformation insurgent and lyric poet, whose French and Spanish connections linked him to wider European networks.[132] For those thirty-eight years, actors from a Gaelic world at the height of its powers, an expansionist England, and the Catholic states of Western Europe lived and fought cheek-by-jowl. The deep map recovers that adjacency.

Jobson assured Burleigh that he had 'discribed and plotted somuch as came to my sight in travellinge 'through' Munster. But there was so much that he never saw, so much that he had little inclination to hear and less ability to comprehend. By reinserting what was 'adjacent' but occluded on Jobson's map, the deep map (re)introduces what the colonial map silenced twice over, first by what it left out and second by the conquest which it enabled: a great lord watching skittish doves at play; a poet imagining wind, moon, birds, fish, and waves praising their Creator; the lament for a land left without 'heir or descendant'.[133] The prize for recovering those voices is that we get rare access to *all* the voices in a war of conquest, to the victors, of course, but also to those who had no reason to believe that their civilisation would, unimaginably, be overthrown. 'How are we to map the ... invisibilities which the English map-maker may have missed?', asks William Smyth in *Map-Making, Landscape and Memory*.[134] And how are we to read and understand that which gets recovered? One answer – our answer – is decolonial deep mapping and juxtapuntal reading.

3.4 Strategies for Reading in the Contiguity Zone

Geography and spatiality are at the heart of deep maps. The actors captured on the MACMORRIS deep map were all *there*, on the ground (though not necessarily at the same time). When Lord Mountjoy writes to Robert Cecil, on 13 November 1601, on a 'Morning as cold as a Stone', he really *is* outside the besieged town of Kinsale, in 'my House of Turf, in which I write this'.[135] There is a similar deictic quality to Sir John Harington's censure of the 'defective fortress' at Duncannon,

> whose ditches are low and narrow and shallow; whose rampart and parapet are low and slender; whose defences are *a forbici* and *in barba*; and, that which is worse, their correspondence hindered by the casemates in the ditch, whose *piazza* is narrow, affording no place for retreat.[136]

---

[132] www.dib.ie/biography/maccarthy-mor-donal-a5138.
[133] www.macmorris.maynoothuniversity.ie/site/130, www.macmorris.maynoothuniversity.ie/site/64, www.macmorris.maynoothuniversity.ie/site/8.
[134] Smyth, *Map-Making*, p.65. [135] www.macmorris.maynoothuniversity.ie/site/48.
[136] www.macmorris.maynoothuniversity.ie/site/172.

On the page, Harington's arts-of-war jargon induces a head-reel; placed on the map, ramparts, parapets, casemates, and *piazze* swim into focus as material objects which Queen Elizabeth's godson is insistently pointing out to us. The accompanying thumbnail, a contemporary map of the promontory and its fort – a map within a map – backs up the grounded specificity of Harington's recollection (see Figure 9).

Conquest and colonisation are all about ground: 'the ground possessed and repossessed';[137] the ground war (including the sieges and military engineering that fascinated Harington), standing one's ground. Some of those on the ground are at home; some are in transit; all are moving across that ground; some are eyeing up the prospect of moving in (and up); some will be moved out. The map offers the chance to sample that dynamic because everyone, native and incomer, is rooted in (or being rooted out of) that ground. This dynamic of fixity and extirpation, displacement, replacement, and uneasy cohabitation, is the dynamic of conquest and colonisation itself. Just as early modern Munster was a theatre of contention and clashing forces, so too is the deep map a place of juxtaposition and encounter. Lords, harpers, bardic poets; planters, propagandists, prospectors; papal emissaries, *veedores-generales*, *capitanes* all jostle for space on the map in the same messy propinquity as they did on the contested terrain of Munster during the last decades of the conquest.

This force field of contested co-occupancy is subtly different to Mary Louise Pratt's bordering concept of the 'contact zone'. Pratt defines contact zones as

> social spaces where cultures meet, clash, and grapple with each other, often in contexts of highly asymmetrical relations of power, such as colonialism, slavery, or their aftermaths as they are lived out in many parts of the world today.[138]

But while 'asymmetry' perfectly describes the relationship between Irish and English in the *post*-plantation colony, it does not capture the knife-edge balance of power that held good right up to the end of the Nine Years War (1603). Munster in the years 1569–1607 might better be called a 'contiguity zone', where two freestanding cultures rub up against each other. Whereas the 'highly asymmetrical relations of power' in the *contact* zone mean that the dominant power exercises a monological monopoly, things are very different in the *contiguity* zone. Contiguity is about proximity – adjacency, alongsideness – rather than hierarchised contact. In the contiguity zone, each culture continues to function relatively independently of the other(s). (The European dimension of the conflict and the military, religious, and cultural contributions of Ireland's

---

[137] Heaney, 'Ocean's Love to Ireland', p.40. [138] Pratt, 'Arts of the Contact Zone', 33–40, 34.

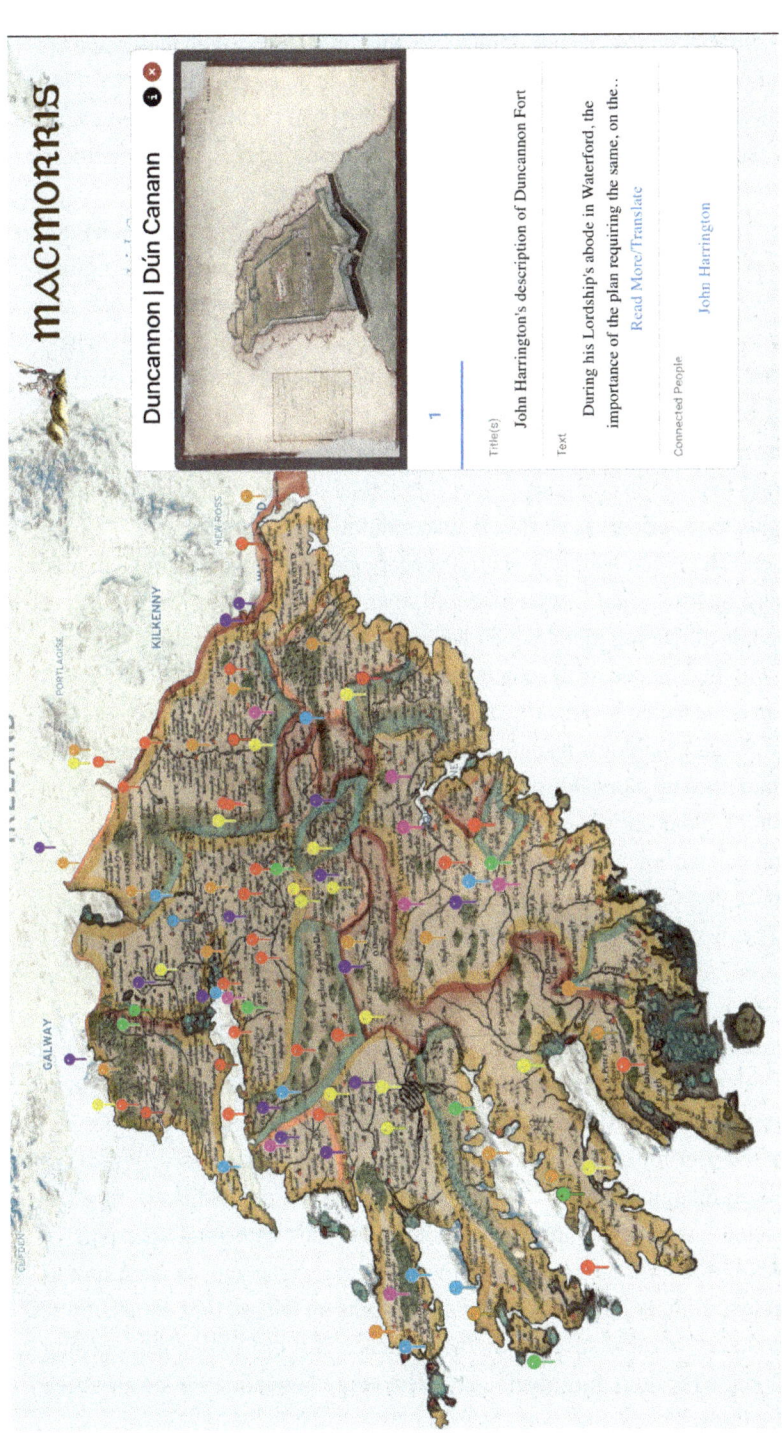

Figure 9 Deep map of Munster (www.macmorris.maynoothuniversity.ie/map)(Duncannon | Dún Canann and snippet view of 'John Harrington's description of Duncannon Fort').

Catholic allies adds a further operational and epistemological layer.) Expression in the contiguity zone is not limited to the imbalanced call and response (command versus complaint/resistance) of a contact zone. Rather, two (and sometimes more) literary, religious, political, and legal traditions – often edgily alert to the machinations of the other – continue to operate independently in uncomfortably close proximity.

The spatiality of the deep map and the pattern of contiguity it captures unlock a new way of reading. The experience of colonisation is disjunctive, disruptive, dislocative. A clash of narratives is so fundamental to its operation that any attempt to reconcile them into a master narrative (in a world where master narratives have long been the preserve of colonialism/coloniality) would be contrary to the decolonising purpose of this deep map. That clash of incommensurate perspectives is literalised by contiguity. Juxtaposition is the form that encounters take in the contiguity zone: it is a zone of contending and intersecting perspectives, of collision, shock, discontinuity, and discordancy. The deep map, therefore, is not simply a neutral display case for the diversified archive assembled by the project's researchers. Rather, the diversifying archive drives the syncopated reading mode which we call 'juxtapuntal'. In seeking to represent all who overlapped on the contested ground of Munster, the MACMORRIS deep map is the fruit of a radically inclusive selection policy. Because it is a deep map and not an anthology, it spatialises the multiple realities and irreconcilable claims that lined up alongside one another in the same space. The organisational principle of 'adjacency' – of texts positioned according to the unmediated geographical fact of proximity, of who is alongside whom or who is in the same space at a different time – allows us to plot a propinquity that is already there. The juxtapuntal reading mode generated by the deep map's spatial organisation answers to juxtapositions produced by incursion and plantation on the ground. Juxtaposition produces a 'transition effect' that draws us sidelong across the map, whether inside a single site populated by disparate actors, or from site to neighbouring site. To click on one map-pin is to be brought to as many as thirteen texts in up to five languages.[139] The logic of the interface prompts the user to toggle through each in turn, cycling successively through texts whose relationship one to another – disjunctive, contradictory, or plain unconnected – captures a plurality and alterity at odds with single-perspective narratives. Following the vector of contiguity, the reader moves from text to adjacent text. Simply by clicking on two map pins on Dingle Bay, for example, one encounters, in rapid succession, the privateer Earl of Cumberland praising Dingle's harpers and 'Chirurgians', a Gaelic elegy lamenting the death of the

---

[139] The aggregation layer allows users to gauge the relative density of extracts at the different sites.

Earl of Clancarthy's only son in French exile, López de Soto's admiring evaluation of Valentia, an English plantation survey, and a natural history of Ireland, in Latin.[140] This spatially realised kaleidoscope of languages, genres, and allegiances means that a wilfully mono-cultural reading would not only be perverse but extremely difficult. A literary scholar hoping to find all Spenserian entries conveniently housed in Kilcolman, for instance, will be sorely disappointed; eighteen extracts from Spenser form part of a multilingual mix in fifteen sites dispersed throughout the province, their coordinates determined by the places in which they were written or to which they referred.[141]

This jostling of perspectives, forms, and languages creates an effect that is, inescapably, jarring. The extracts do not function like jigsaw pieces that the reader can fit together to create a single, unitary picture. There is no hidden narrative subtending these selections, requiring only the ingenuity of the reader to reassemble them into coherence. What is captured in the deep map's intercutting extracts is difference, diversity, incommensurability; the effect is one of syncopation rather than blending or braiding. Each extract was selected on its own terms, whether for its specific aesthetic, informational, site-specific, or quirky qualities. They are not set up as binary pairings of colonised and coloniser, where English and Irish are presented as *recto* to the other's *verso*. Inevitably, there will be echoes across extracts; sometimes, a sequence can be inferred. Domhnall Mac Bruaideadha's entrancing evocation of Pádraigín Mac Muiris's castle in Listowel –

> an chuirt g[h]roighigh ghealmhóir ghloin,
> seanróimh oinigh an íarthair (41.3-4);

> the fair bright court, wide and full of steeds,
> old sanctuary of the honour of the west

– is juxtaposed with Charles Wilmot's account of making a 'bed ready to place the powder' required to blow the castle up.[142] But mostly the extracts, for all the contiguity of their placing, are records not of a face-off but of discontinuity. Each freeze-frames a moment of particularity. Together, they capture the dissonance of a bitter and brutal encounter. What they don't provide is the dispersed elements of some phantom unified, sequential story. Instead, juxtaposition works as a form of montage. While sometimes sharing an occasion, these texts operate independently of one another, coexisting in a shared space but not directly 'in dialogue' with one another. Moreover, as one of the greatest

---

[140] See sites 53, 129, 166, 132, 192, in Dingle and Valentia.
[141] Bourke, 'Deep Mapping Spenser in Munster'.
[142] www.macmorris.maynoothuniversity.ie/site/15 and www.macmorris.maynoothuniversity.ie/site/39.

contemporary exponents of montage, John Akomfrah, reminds us, montage isn't just a technique but 'an ethic'. It is an ethic focused on

> the way in which one accepted the coexistence of difference ... the idea that things which are seemingly mutually exclusive from different worlds, things with different ontologies almost, can be brought into a relationship. No more than that, just a relationship to each other.[143]

As montage can bring texts from different worlds and different ontologies together, complexity and depth can be added to the deep map by facilitating different patterns of montage. One way we achieved this was through the use of filtering. Since each of the textual sections are categorised into one of seven categories, an interactive filter allows users to choose how many categories are active on the map at any moment. When the map first loads, all seven categories are active and users can explore the full extent of the contiguity zone. However, users can also choose to select either a single category (or several), which creates multiple non-linear thematic assemblages for exploration. The filters create, effectively, clusters of bounded juxtapositions. Since no category is made up of only colonial or Gaelic perspectives, nothing can filter out multiplicity. Robertson and Mullen highlight that 'the path that one takes through the deep map constitutes the meaning that one makes from it', and navigating the MACMORRIS deep map by activating the filters does something similar, without the directiveness of a 'path'.[144] Each selection activates the ethic of montage: each delimited category demonstrates 'the coexistence of difference'.[145] If, for example, a user filters by 'conflict and violence', he or she is presented with fifty-nine texts mapped to thirty-seven different locations (see Figure 10). These include references to the sacking of Kilmallock in the *Annals of the Four Masters* alongside references to George Carew's capturing of Dunboy in the *Pacata Hibernia*.[146] The user still needs to engage with the extracts' different ontologies and the map's non-linear presentation. As the filters do not impose an order in which to engage with the narrowed-down textual selection, filtering does not close off the potential for multiple stories. It simply limits the number of arrangements that can be created at that specific moment. Furthermore, the hovering presence of the other categories on the margin of the map constantly signals that there are alternative selections and arrangements, all of which offer different ways to build stories from juxtapositions and, as we see in the next section, engage with the time zone of the deep map.

---

[143] Løgstrup, *The Contemporary Condition*, p.9.
[144] Robertson and Mullen, 'Navigating through Narrative', p. 134.
[145] Løgstrup, *The Contemporary Condition*, p.9.
[146] https://macmorris.maynoothuniversity.ie/site/24; https://macmorris.maynoothuniversity.ie/site/186.

Figure 10 Deep map of Munster (www.macmorris.maynoothuniversity.ie/map) (Map with 'conflict and violence' filter selected).

3.5 The Time Zone of Deep Mapping

Contiguity, and the arrangement of texts spatially, in line with the testy 'adjacency' of antagonists in a time of conflict, makes available the materials for juxtapuntal readings. But spatiality has significant temporal implications as well. The form works against linearity – against beginnings, middles, and ends. It offers, therefore, time out from the usual teleological reading of the period, where events unfold inexorably towards a conclusion that is seen – but, always, only retrospectively – as inevitable: 'the collapse of the Gaelic order' and the ascendancy the New English colony. But there was nothing inevitable about the English victory at Kinsale and, with it, the overthrow of Gaelic resistance. Fynes Moryson, who served as Lord Mountjoy's secretary throughout the campaign, and was with him on 'the durty fields before Kinsale',[147] could scarcely bring himself to recall how close the English came to defeat:

> In this last rebellion I am afraid to remember how little that kingdom wanted of being lost and rent from the English Government, for it was not a small disturbance of peace or a light trouble of the state, but the very foundations of the English power in that kingdom were shaken and fearfully tottered, and were preserved from ruin more by the Providence of God out of His great mercy (as may appear by the particular affairs at the siege of Kinsale) than by our counsels and remedies (which were in the beginning full of negligence, in the progress distracted with strong factions, and to the end slow and sparing in all supplies).[148]

Central to MACMORRIS's reading strategy, therefore, is an attempt to disable teleology on the utopian third space of the deep map. Here, its resistance to providing narrative pathways through the text comes into focus once again as a decolonising imperative. Robertson and Mullen emphasise the centrality of chronology in plotting pathways through deep maps:

> Narrative ... partakes of the fundamental acts of historical thinking. It selects the materials that will comprise the narrative. It arranges them to make meaning out of them. In many instances it periodizes them as a part of telling that story, thus contributing to the shaping of historical knowledge.

A 'spatial narrative assumes that proximity in space, just like ordered chronology in time, is related to causation'.[149] Periodisation, causation, selection, and the very 'shaping of historical knowledge' all play into a colonial teleology which sees the colonist marching into modernity and the colonised slinking back into the left-behind temporality of the 'pre-'. This is the colonial

---

[147] Gainsford, *The True Exemplary, and Remarkable History of the Earle of Tirone*, A2.
[148] Moryson, *The Commonwealth of Ireland*, p. 289.
[149] Robertson and Mullen, 'Navigating through Narrative', p. 135.

equivalent of the denial of coevalness, the refusal to see the Other as an epistemological contemporary, which Johannes Fabian ascribes to anthropological discourse.[150] The spatiality of the deep map, however, and the contiguity it captures, privileges 'coevalness' by its very nature. On the deep map, each extract constitutes a *punctum temporis*. Each is an event in itself, arrested its own particularity, and encountered on its own terms rather than as an episode in a larger, steamrolling chronology. The capacity of deep mapping to provide a counterweight to the inevitably one-sided trajectory of colonial history is central to MACMORRIS's decolonial ethic. It's worth pausing here, therefore, to examine how it creates arrested moments and enables a mode of navigation between each *punctum* which is resistant to teleology.

First, let's look at how the deep map freeze-frames moments in time and, in doing so, disrupts unexamined presumptions of sequentiality. When Baothgalach Mac Flannchadha writes to Sir Richard Bingham from the 'Fields of Liscannor', on 6 September 1588, breathlessly reporting that 'Last night two ships were seen about the islands of Arran', we catch him frozen in that instant of breaking news. The 'cockboat ... painted red, with the red anchor' which has just been spotted is a first sighting of the Armada.[151] The map pin at Spanish Point, just down the coast, leads the reader into the very different temporality of retrospection, when the *Annals of the Four Masters* chronicle that 'Great numbers of the Spaniards were drowned, and their ships were totally wrecked' ('Ro báidheadh dronga móra do na Spainneachaibh is na hoirearaibh sin iar láinbhriseadh a long').[152] The thumbnail from John Speed's *The Invasions of England and Ireland* at the same site occupies an unstable temporal point somewhere between the two reports. It shows four ships in various stages of foundering – drifting, broken-masted, listing, sinking. The effect is less of four distinct ships, each coincidentally caught in a different stage of distress, than of the same ship captured in time-lapse, where the successive stages are represented simultaneously. A second extract at Spanish Point, from Book 5 of *The Faerie Queene*, brings us to yet another temporality, that of allegory. The scattering of the Armada is transmogrified into the chivalric combat of romance, during which Arthur and Artegall pitilessly toss the Souldan

> Quite topside turuey, and the pagan hound
> Amongst the yron hookes and graples keene,
> [Is] Torne all to rags.[153]

Allegory extracts – and abstracts – actual events from the flow of history. In what Gordon Teskey calls allegory's 'project of capture',[154] a real-world

---

[150] Fabian, *Time and the Other*. [151] www.macmorris.maynoothuniversity.ie/site/111.
[152] www.macmorris.maynoothuniversity.ie/site/107.
[153] www.macmorris.maynoothuniversity.ie/site/198. [154] Teskey, *Allegory and Violence*, p.8.

happening is turned into 'historicall fiction', and spun off into the *Faerie Queene*'s dreamlike, providential, and bewildering timespace.

As we see, several temporalities are at work here, all militating against unitary narratives and notions of linear progression. There is the undirected and therefore random order in which the reader chooses to click onto the different extracts, a sequence most likely at odds with the actual timeline on which events unfolded (first the sightings, then the sinkings). Each textual fragment represents a moment of particularity extracted from the continuum of historical time. But, as the Armada extracts show, the different time signature of each extract is shaped by the genre in which it is told – live-action witness reportage, the post-factum fixity of chronicle, the translation of current affairs into the affected 'timelessness' of allegorical romance.

As the Armada examples suggest, therefore, the deep map's assemblage of manifold genres multiplies timespaces. But the proliferation of genres across the deep map doesn't just multiply points of view and modes of apprehending the world (a bardic poem, for example, apprehends nature very differently to a plantation survey). It multiplies chronotopes as well. For Bakhtin, the chronotope 'expresses the inseparability of space and time' in literature:

> Time, as it were, thickens, takes on flesh, becomes artistically visible; likewise, space becomes charged and responsive to the movements of time, plot and history.

Bakhtin's 'notes toward a historical poetics' focus on literary texts, but '[t]he process of assimilating real historical time and space' into non-fiction texts creates just as much of a time signature.[155] So, on the deep map we have the altogether discrepant and incomparable temporality of prayer, military dispatch, epic, natural history, satire. We have personal, lyric time:

> But be it so or not, the effects are past;
> Her love hath end; my woe must ever last.[156]

We have the sacred time of the Resurrection:

> A mheic Mhuire gidh mac mná
> dá mbeith gan luighe fán lia
> ní fiú an uile bhur n-eacht rú
> tú ag teacht ad dhuine 's ad Dhia;
>
> O son of Mary, though son of a woman,
> your journey would not have been worth it all

---

[155] Bakhtin, 'Forms of Time and of the Chronotope in the Novel', pp.84–85.
[156] Walter Ralegh's 'The Ocean to Cynthia', placed at Lismore: www.macmorris.maynoothuniversity.ie/site/177.

> were you not to lie under the headstone
> [and] return as a man and as a God.[157]

We have the temporality of the dashed-off letter:

> Yo llegué tan tarde a este castillo que casi no podré dar entera satisfacción por la falta de luz que aquí hay hasta que venga la mañana;
>
> I arrived at this castle so late that, for want of light, I will not be able to give an entirely satisfactory report about what's here until morning comes.[158]

The diversity of the assemblage, the plurality of cultural formations, forms, and languages, and the riot of chronotopes they unleash militate against the notion of a simple chronology. This is not an assemblage where each event can be allocated its slot on a fixed timeline. That temporal complexity is redoubled when the texts assembled are spatialised on the deep map. Then, it is not just chronology that falters: it is teleology itself. On the flat plane of the deep map, time, too, gets flattened. The red button on the MACMORRIS's homepage enjoining us to 'EXPLORE MAP!' brings us to a gently rotating map of Munster. When the map rocks to a halt, there are no more instructions, just coloured map pins inviting us to click on one – *any* one. The sequence chosen will be individual, random, unpredictable; users' freewheeling, undirected, recursive movements from map pin to map pin open up potentially endless, recombinant permutations. Despite the thirty-eight-year span of the texts assembled, on the deep map everything is happening all at once. Toirdhealbhach Ruadh Mac Mathghamhna is 'dwelling in Thomond beside the Shannon'.[159] The De Búrca are sailing between '[b]ord Siúire na sreabhán mbinn', 'the banks of the Suir of sweet-sounding streamlets'.[160] The Sugán Earl is being entertained by a harper – 'almost ready to goe to supper' – when the household is surprised by soldiers and forced to flee, leaving 'their meate ... and a mantle' behind.[161] No one event has temporal priority over the others.

The mixture of particularity and simultaneity intrinsic to the deep map – each extract is encountered on its own terms, freeze-framed in its own specificity; and all exist on the same flattened temporal plane – locates them in a temporal zone quite outside the continuum of history. The distinction is similar to that between *kairos* (καιρός) and *chronos* (χρόνος). 'Whereas *chronos* denotes a linear and progressive sense of time, *kairos* stands in opposition as a rare singularity ... a deviation from linear and universal time.'[162] It is the time of

---

[157] www.macmorris.maynoothuniversity.ie/site/141.
[158] www.macmorris.maynoothuniversity.ie/site/162.
[159] www.macmorris.maynoothuniversity.ie/site/120.
[160] www.macmorris.maynoothuniversity.ie/site/70.
[161] www.macmorris.maynoothuniversity.ie/site/49.
[162] Paul, 'The Use of *Kairos* in Renaissance Political Philosophy', 43–78, 47.

'the radically particular'.[163] The deep-map extracts, unmoored from the fixity of chronology, are temporarily at least, detached from unitary narratives that rely on linear progression. Of course, the end can't be held in suspense forever: the castles will fall, the poets will find no takers for their poems, their patrons will die on the battlefield or flee into exile, the new colonial order will have its day. But the deep map stops the clock and, as long as it is stopped, everything is still in play. 'Before' and 'after' don't have coordinates on this spatial plane. If we click on the map in at Glanageenty, from where the severed head of Gearóid Mac Gearailt, the 15th Earl of Desmond, was despatched to London, we will find Donnchadh Mac Craith elegising his dead leader:

> A chinn mo ríogh ráinig soir
> ó Shliabh Luachra go Lunndoin
> do-dhéana mé, a chinn mo chroidhe,
> mo ré rinn na heólchuire;

> O head of my heart, o head of my king which went east from Sliabh Luachra to London, I will spend [the rest of] my life on the spike of grief.[164]

But if we move the cursor just a fraction to the right, eastwards to Sliabh Luachra, we will find William Pelham irritably reporting that 'The Earl of Desmond, the Countess, and [Fr.] Sanders ... escaped hardly, the priest being fane to leave his gown behind him'.[165] In the Schrödinger's-cat world of the deep map, Desmond is both dead and has, however narrowly, made good his escape.

In the arrested, all-together, all-at-once temporality of the deep map, teleology is kept at bay. The conquest is not complete; the Gaelic world may be embattled but is still flourishing. The Spanish have landed. An Italian captain notes that 'Tam viri quam foeminae sese osculantur, quando primum occurran', 'As many men as women kiss one another on the lips when first they meet'.[166] It is to the multifaceted world of the contiguity zone we next turn, to see where it takes us when read juxtapuntally.

4 Juxtapuntal Readings: Mapping Counter-Discourses

At Cluain Mín on the northern banks of the River Blackwater, the map pin brings us to two extracts (see Figure 11). The first is a joint elegy for Domhnall

---

[163] Miller, 'Foreword', xiii. Safet Hadžimuhamedović, analysing what he calls the 'schizochronotopia' of 'The Field' in post-war Bosnia, similarly distinguishes between 'qualitative' time, calqued on kairatic time, and 'critical' time, i.e. the temporality that is 'qualitative and linear, like *kronos*'. It seems entirely appropriate, therefore, that he describes his work as 'a form of "deep mapping"'; see *Waiting for Elijah*, p.57, p.5.
[164] www.macmorris.maynoothuniversity.ie/site/138.
[165] www.macmorris.maynoothuniversity.ie/site/34.
[166] www.macmorris.maynoothuniversity.ie/site/151.

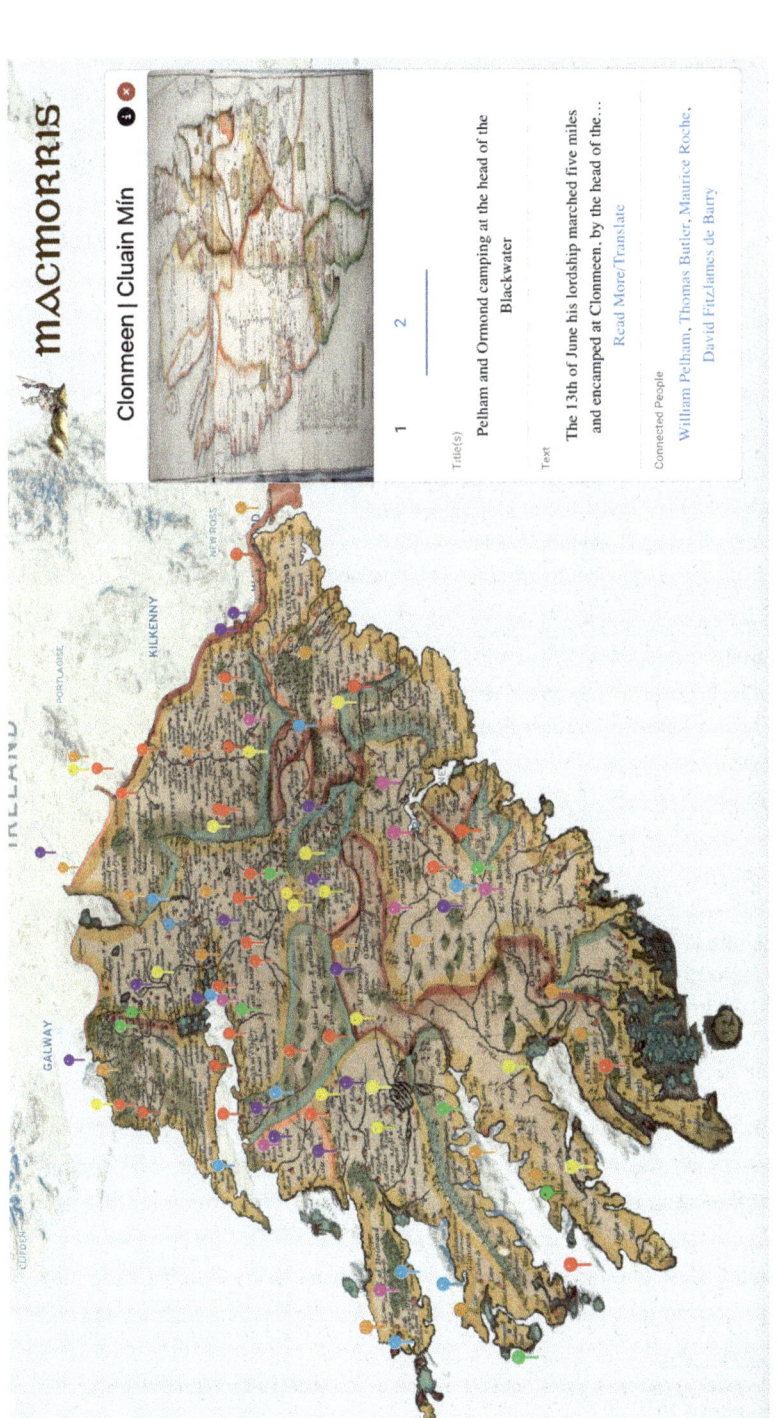

Figure 11 Deep map of Munster (www.macmorris.maynoothuniversity.ie/map)(Clonmeen | Cluain Mín and snippet view of 'Pelham and Ormond camping at the head of the Blackwater').

Ó Caoimh, chief of his name, and the poet who once eulogised him, Aonghus Ó Dálaigh Fionn. Ó Caoimh garnered scarcely a mention in English sources but, in Irish, he was celebrated for the cultural vibrancy of his lordship. Over several generations, the Ó Caoimh were associated with the Ó Dálaigh Fionn bardic school at Nuachabháil Uí Dhálaigh. Now, in his elegy, Fear Feasa Ó'n Cháinte memorialises that connection, remembering Ó Dálaigh for 'awakening delight, studying bundles of bright and faultless scrolls'[167] and Ó Caoimh for his hospitality to young scholar-poets:

> Ní bhíodh sgolaidhe don sgail
> dá mbíodh i mbaile Í Dhálaigh
> gan chomaoin éigin ón fhior
> d'fhor raoin nar bh'éidir d'áiriomh.
>
> Chuige do ghabhdaois trá ag teacht,
> do bhídís aige ag imtheacht
> go hionbhuidh sgaoilte don sgail,
> faoilte ionmhuin re a n-aghaidh;

Of the scholars at Ó Dálaigh's home there was no one who didn't get a gift from the hero, not one of that numerous band!

On their arrival they would visit him, at their departure they would come to him, a kind welcome awaiting them till the time of the school-term's ending.[168]

The second extract comes from Captain William Pelham's campaign journal and, in switching to it, that Gaelic world of culture and conviviality vanishes, as though it had never existed:

> The 13th of June his lordship marched five miles and encamped at Clonmeen, by the head of the River of Blackwater that enters the sea below Youghal. The Earl of Ormond encamped not far off. The Lords Barry and Roche came to his lordship, betwixt who appeared great enmity, which my lord (with persuading them to come together in service) promised to reform.[169]

From Pelham's perspective, Clonmeen is a nowhere place, a temporary encampment on the banks of a river flowing somewhere else. The captain would strike camp next morning with no awareness of his proximity to a rich cultural ecosystem that lay entirely beyond his ken.

By laying these two incommensurate world views side by side, the deep map opens the door to juxtapuntal readings. In confronting us with what lay beyond

---

[167] 'léaghadh meall nglanrolla ngeal, / ceann foghloma na bhfileadh': www.macmorris.maynoothuniversity.ie/site/20.
[168] www.macmorris.maynoothuniversity.ie/site/156.
[169] www.macmorris.maynoothuniversity.ie/site/200.

the purview of the English text, the juxtaposition enables us to see what Pelham didn't. To read juxtapuntally is, metaphorically, to do the very opposite of striking camp and marching on to the next colonial text. Instead, it gives us a methodology for going beyond the range of colonial perception – censuring, uncomprehending, and deprecative – and rescuing what Arturo Escobar calls 'non-hegemonic and silenced counter-discourses'.[170] As a counter-map of colonial cartography, the MACMORRIS deep map is, by extension, a counter-map to colonial epistemology. To be truly decolonising, however, it must do two things. On the one hand, it must fulfil what Manuela Boatcă identifies as a key decolonial strategy: it must create 'a relational perspective capable of revealing the constitutive entanglements through which a global capitalism grounded in colonial expansion interlinked all areas of the world'.[171] On the other hand, and most importantly, it must *re*-place the subalternised complexity of Gaelic culture on the level playing field of a deep map. In bringing what was elided and repressed by conquest and colonisation back into play, it does not simply challenge English assertions; much more valuably, it reintroduces perspectives *exterior* to the discourse of proto-modernity that England was concept-testing in early modern Ireland. The rest of this section explores the possibilities of juxtapuntal reading for two crucial literary domains, Comparative Literature and Ecocriticism.

4.1 Decolonising Comparative Literature

The deep map's multilingual assemblage makes available the discrepant testimonies of individuals living cheek-by-jowl in Munster's theatre of conquest and plantation. By recovering this multi-voiced record in line with the very real contiguity of the original encounter, texts from different languages and domains rub shoulders in a way that makes comparative readings inescapable. When anglophone works that have had the floor for so long have to share the stage with works speaking a very different truth, the scene is set for *decolonised* comparative readings. The resultant clash of perspectives and sensibilities makes juxtapuntal readings unavoidable. Risam's concern that the 'fissures and lacunae' which are 'the hallmarks of colonialism in the cultural record ... are being ported over into the digital cultural record, unthinkingly'[172] speaks also to the field of Comparative Literature. If digital literary studies have been slow to move beyond canonical texts in languages amplified by empire, comparative literature struggles similarly to bring texts from outside languages elevated to 'world-language' status only by colonialism into scholarly conversations.[173] Comparative Literature rarely

---

[170] Escobar, 'Worlds and Knowledges Otherwise', 187.
[171] Boatcă, 'Counter-Mapping as Method', 246.   [172] Risam, *New Digital Worlds*, p.5.
[173] Even groundbreaking work like David Damrosch's *Comparing the Literatures*, focuses on works that are canonical in their respective literary traditions.

Figure 12 Deep map of Munster (www.macmorris.maynoothuniversity.ie/map) (Carrick-on-Suir | Carraig na Siúire and snippet view of 'Spenser's celebration of Butler').

finds space for literary traditions marginalised by imbalances of power – traditions now seen as occupying a realm of alien or unfamiliar conventions, genres, influences, canons, and social function. Recognising the quandary, Susan Bassnett asks 'what new directions in comparative literature [can] there be for the European scholar whose intellectual formation has been shaped by ... generations of [European] writers who have borrowed, translated, plagiarised and plundered' from the rest of the world?[174] The answer, the deep map suggests, may lie in engaging with works which testify to quite literal 'plunder' very close to home.

To see how a more linguistically plural approach to digital literary studies nudges comparative readings in a decolonial direction, let's go to just one site of the deep map, Carrick-on-Suir, seat of Thomas Butler, 10th Earl of Ormond (see Figure 12).

The order in which extracts appear is determined, randomly, by coding, rather than by any editorial decision, and first up is Edmund Spenser's dedicatory sonnet to Ormond from *The Faerie Queene*:

> Receiue most noble Lord a simple taste
> Of the wilde fruit, which saluage soyl hath bred.
> Which being through long wars left almost waste,
> With brutish barbarisme is ouerspredd:
> And in so faire a land, as may be redd
> Not one Parnassus, nor one Helicone

---

[174] Bassnett, 'Reflections on Comparative Literature in the Twenty-First Century', 3–11, 4–5.

> Left for sweete Muses to be harboured.
> But where thy selfe hast thy braue mansione;
> There in deede dwel faire Graces many one.
> And gentle Nymphes, delights of learned wits,
> And in thy person without Paragone
> All goodly bountie and true honour sits,
> Such therefore, as that wasted soyl doth yield,
> Receiue dear Lord in worth, the fruit of barren field.[175]

'[W]ilde fruit', 'saluage soyl', 'brutish barbarisme': for the moment, let's just leave the familiar tropes marinating there, and pass on to the next extract, Pistol's exchange with a French gentleman in *Henry V*. At one level, it brings us to Agincourt, but it also returns us, circuitously, to the River Suir, which flows past Ormond's Elizabethan manor:

> PISTOL Yield, cur!
> FRENCH SOLDIER *Je pense que vous êtes le gentilhommede bonne qualité.*
> PISTOL *Qualité?* '*Caleno custore me*'!
> Art thou a gentleman? What is thy name? Discuss.
> FRENCH SOLDIER *O Seigneur Dieu!*
> PISTOL O Signieur Dew should be a gentleman.[176]

Shakespeare's hammed-up hodgepodge of linguistic confusion sits comfortably in a deep map which generates its own kind of Babel. *Henry V*, a play rather more focused on the Nine Years War than the Hundred Years' War, as its reference to Essex 'from Ireland coming, / Bringing rebellion broached on his sword' (5.0.31-32) shows, stands front and centre as an English canonical text that has been made to speak for Ireland. Indeed, a disquiet about literary critics' readiness to seize on *Henry V* as the go-to text when discussing Ireland – a country and a conflict it is more inclined to scoff at than understand – was an early impetus for the MACMORRIS project.[177] The project's name, in ironically doffing its hat to Shakespeare's stage-Irish character, signals its intention to provide some answers to Captain Macmorris irate questions: 'What ish my nation? Who talks of my nation?' (3.2.123). The deep map ensures that those answers come from several directions at once, in several languages, including, crucially, the mother tongue ghosting the irascible captain's broken English.

One man's 'gibberish' can, of course, be another man's lyric and so it is with Pistol's. The third extract at Carrick quotes the very line which Pistol reproduced as 'Caleno custore me' and restores it to sense. A writer whose name

---

[175] www.macmorris.maynoothuniversity.ie/site/56.
[176] www.macmorris.maynoothuniversity.ie/site/140.
[177] Palmer, 'Missing Bodies' and Palmer, Baker, and Maley, 'What Ish My Network?'

was once known folds the title of a popular harp tune, 'Chailín ó chois tSiúire mé', 'I'm a girl from the banks of the Siur', into a playful love poem or *dán grádh*:

> Dom anródh nár fhoghlaim mé
> seinm chailín ó chois tSiúire,
> i dtráth suain le sreing n-umha,
> nách beinn uaidh i n-aontumha (8);
>
> Sás na mban maith do mhealladh –
> cuid dá ríomh do rinneamar –
> puirt luatha [ar] a gcluinim cion;
> sguirim uatha dá n-áireamh.
>
> I did not learn from my anguish –
> the playing of 'Cailín ó chois tSiúire [mé]' –
> at bedtime from copper strings,
> I would not give it up for a life of celibacy.
>
> The instrument of women, good for enticing,
> lively tunes in which I hear affection –
> I counted some of them –
> I give up counting them.

The refrain which Pistol deploys as a monoglots's 'rhubarb-rhubarb' to distract from his ignorance of French, here, functions as a *passe partout* to the coterie world of the *dánta grádha*, characterised by wit, musicality, role-playing, and world-weary sophistication.

The fourth extract brings us to *Ormonius*, the Neo-Latin heroic poem which celebrates the 10th Earl's military career, across five books and almost 4000 hexameters. Written by Dermot O'Meara, Thomas Butler's physician, this 'spectacular example of classical influence on Irish letters and politics' is itself a major work of cultural and linguistic syncretism.[178] Self-consciously Virgilian in its celebration of Butler's *pietas* and military prowess, it sits equally comfortably within the Gaelic tradition of the *caithréim*, or 'battle roll', recapitulating its hero's campaigns (crushing Wyatt in England, the Macdonalds' in Scotland, Desmond in Munster, and – wishful-thinkingly – O'Neill in the Nine Years War).[179] O'Meara brings the full panoply of classical epic – its locations, imagery, gods, personifications, even a psychopomp from the kingdom of the dead – to the banks of the Suir:

---

[178] Kane, 'Sidwell and Edwards, eds. "The Tipperary Hero: Dermot O'Meara's *Ormonius* (1615)"'.
[179] For examples of an actual Gaelic *caithréim* dedicated to Ormond, see www.macmorris.maynoothuniversity.ie/site/29 and www.macmorris.maynoothuniversity.ie/site/30.

> Condignos hic ille diu dum carpit honores,
> Tristia cimerias linquit penetralia valles
> Mopheus: hoc illi rector superûmque hominumque
> Imperat; et nullos strepitus facientibus alis
> Per tenebras volitans, intra breve tempus in urbem
> Londini vehitur, positisque e corpore pennis,
> Faemineam adsimulat faciem, tellusque Dynastae
> Ormonio apparens Hyberna: his solverat ora:
> 'Nate decus, viresque meae, mea gloria magna ....';
>
> While Ormond here for long received due praise,
> Morpheus relinquished the Cimmerian Vale,
> His grim abode (thus had his order come
> From the controller of both gods and men).
> His wings were silent as he flitted through
> The darkness and within a little space
> Was borne to London city, where he laid
> Aside his body's feathers and put on
> A female face, appearing as the land
> Hibernia to the dynast Ormond. Thus
> He spoke: 'My honoured son, my glory great ...'[180]

The final extract at this geolocation, *Taghaim Tómás ragha is róghrádh*, was written around 1588 by another poet whose name has not survived. It is an exuberant example of the Gaelic genre of 'castle poetry', though not written in the classical syllabic form, *dán díreach*. In that, it is as innovative as the building it celebrates. Ormond renovated his castle in the 1570s, adding the long gallery which Stephen Brindle calls 'one of the most beautiful rooms in Ireland', hoping that it might tempt the Queen to visit.[181] The energy of Ormond's regional nerve centre is captured in a riot of anaphora and alliterating adjectives:

> cúirt gan toirse, cúirt na soillse,
> cúirt 'na coinnleach céir-thapuir;
> bláthbhrugh biadhmhur plástrach piasdach
> gabhlach grianach gréasthallach.
>
> Finnteagh fleadhach slinnteach sleaghach
> geimhleach greaghach géibheannach;
> ceólbhrugh cluthair bordghlan bruthmhur
> córnach cupach craobhdhathach,
> fionbhrugh féasdach buidhneach béasach
> daoineach déarcach daorchoimtheach;

---

[180] www.macmorris.maynoothuniversity.ie/site/149.
[181] Brindle, *Architecture in Britain and Ireland: 1530–1830*.

> teaghdhais taithneamhach dhearrsgnach dhealbhach
> áluinn amlach aol-chreatach;
>
> court without sorrow, court of lights,
> court of cere-tapered candles;
> polished, bountiful mansion, serpentinely stuccoed,
> branching, sunshiny, with ornamented walls.
>
> Bright seat, slated, welcoming, weaponed
> holding hostages, horses, and prisoners;
> sheltering, strong-walled music-mansion of polished tables
> goblets, drinking horns in coloured interlace
> festive, triumphant, cultivated wine-hall
> humane, benevolent, protector of the low-born
> pleasant, burnished, shapely dwelling
> lovely, adorned, lime-bodied.[182]

Malcolm Kelsall pounced on the middle lines of Spenser's dedicatory sonnet to Ormond (the opening extract at Carrick-on-Suir) and declared it to be 'the first Irish country-house poem in English'.[183] Merely to compare Spenser's 'embryonic' country-house poem (if we lower the generic bar sufficiently to call it such) –

> where thy selfe hast thy braue mansione:
> There in deede dwel faire Graces many one.
> And gentle Nymphes, delights of learned wits

– with the Gaelic castle poem we have just looked is to unlock new, decolonising possibilities for comparative literature.[184] Irish castle poetry, like all of these other Irish and Latin works, takes us deep inside a culture which English observers could only guess at (and project onto) from the outside. That is the place of alterity from which juxtapuntal reading does its decolonial work.

4.2 Decolonial Comparative Eco-Criticism

Now, as the world crashes through the safe limits of most earth systems, we need more than ever to respond to the decolonial imperative to recover perspectives that run counter to the discourses of exploitation and mastery pioneered in early modernity. Ireland's conquest and colonisation coincided (and not by accident) with the period when the world was being remade and unmade, climatically and biologically, by convulsive transformations like intensified agriculture, the emergence of mercantile capitalism, European colonisation overseas, the first globalisation, and the rise of the slave

---

[182] www.macmorris.maynoothuniversity.ie/site/4.
[183] Kelsall, *Literary Representations of the Irish Country House*, p.18.
[184] Palmer, 'The Gaelic Court and Country House Poetry', 65–85.

trade.[185] These processes were intimately connected. Embedded even in Ludolf von Münchhausen's facetious travelogue are pointers to that larger historical picture, as when he tells us that 'there happened to be a ship full of negroes in Ireland, which had been intercepted at sea, at this time'. His casual segue from the all-male pilgrimage site of Móin na hInse (where a woman was turned to stone for daring to crash a patriarchal enclave) to the human cargo of the Middle Passage – 'there happened to be' – leaves the wider context of imperial expansion (and great-power competition: 'intercepted at sea') unexplained. His flirtation with the idea that he might '*buy* one of the negresses and bring her to the island in man's clothes', to live-test whether a woman entering the island would indeed turn to stone, demonstrates just how ambient and naturalised a presumed entitlement to exploitation was.[186] But if the deep map platforms emergent discourses that herald a convulsive entry into proto-modernity, such as von Münchhausen's racialising empiricism, its juxtapuntal nature means that is simultaneously stages a cacophonous face-off with what Escobar calls 'knowledges otherwise'. As mentioned in Section 3, the deep map's filter function allows users to select particular thematic foci. So, by selecting the blue and green map layers the user gains access to discourses which stored very different ways of engaging with the world – lifeways and ontologies which were now, suddenly, endangered (see Figure 13). Between them, they provide material for a twin-track decolonial eco-criticism, by making available both the emergent discourses of early capitalism and the soon-to-be eclipsed perspectives of a pre-capitalist world.

In *Local Histories/Global Designs*, Walter Mignolo advocated for '*mundialización*' as a strategy for restoring the diversity of world views flattened by colonisation and the globalisation of coloniality.[187] Shortly afterwards, in *Death of a Discipline*, Gayatri Chakravorty Spivak called for a 'new comparative literature' that would resist globalisation by embracing what she called 'planetarity'. For Spivak, 'planetarity' entails reimagining a relationship between the human and the natural worlds that is 'in excess' of modern capitalist globalisation – a relationship for which the 'pre-capitalist cultures of the planet' provide a model.[188] Early modern Ireland is fascinating precisely because a highly articulate pre-capitalist culture came up against a culture in the throes of shaping and articulating (not least through practical experimentation in Ireland) a new, proto-capitalist way of being in the world. That clash means that 'the Tudor experiment in (language) extinction and (territorial) extraction makes Ireland the ideal laboratory for a form of ecological dispossession that

---

[185] For a global history of the process, see Amrith, *The Burning Earth*.
[186] www.macmorris.maynoothuniversity.ie/site/152; our emphasis.
[187] Mignolo, *Local Histories/Global Designs*. [188] Spivak, *Death of a Discipline*, p.72, p.101.

Figure 13 Deep map of Munster (www.macmorris.maynoothuniversity.ie/map)(Map with 'blue' and 'green' filters selected).

will be replayed endlessly in various corners of the Empire'.[189] Radically new conceptions of ownership and property ('surrender and re-grant' which replaced Irish collective land holding with private property, the enclosure of the commons, confiscation, and plantation), the suppression of Brehon Law and the imposition of Common Law, new ethnically defined theories and practices of social segregation, new military technologies, new concepts and practices of 'individuality' and 'privacy', and a dramatically altered relationship with the land and its provisions – all were field-tested in Ireland before being adapted for application elsewhere.[190] There, happening in real time, we can follow 'the radical reconversion of human and biophysical ecologies' into 'resources'[191] and, just as vividly, we can re-encounter compelling counter discourses that would have to be minoritised and discredited for the emerging discourses of the Anthropocene to carry the day.

All across the deep map, we see that clash of world views being played out. On the one hand, we find an expansionist language of prospecting, where the acquisition of land through violence and its assistive scientific and discursive technologies (land surveying and legal sleights of hand) are inseparable from the commodification of nature. On the other, we meet discourses which would be seen off by those very forces but which can, amid the climate and biodiversity crises of the present,[192] offer resources for imagining more sustainable engagements with the earth. A cluster of extracts speak in the accents of the new, instrumental dispensation, geared to exploiting natural 'resources'. Its underpinning grammar is, of course, greed. Sir William Herbert, grantee of the largest seignory in Kerry, writes to Lord Burleigh to petition for more:

> For that I mean to take but 6,000 acres within the county of Kerry, and am desirous to have other 6,000 acres in the county of Desmond, after the Earl of Clancarr's death, I beseech your honourable favour and furtherance to Her Majesty that I may there have Castle logh, the Pallace, and Ballicarbry, with 6,000 acres of land about them. I write thus timely lest some other should first make suit for them.[193]

Before our eyes, we see land itself being turned into a market commodity. The anonymous author whom Richard Hakluyt included in *The Principal Navigations* – reminding us that conquering Ireland fitted within the larger

---

[189] Cronin, *An Ghaeilge agus An Éirceolaíocht – Irish and Ecology*, p.11.
[190] For a discussion of the wider context, Bhandar, *Colonial Lives of Property*; Latour, *We Have Never Been Modern*; Lewis and Maslin, *The Human Planet*.
[191] Escobar, 'Worlds and Knowledges Otherwise', 198.
[192] On how we can use early modernity to think through the crises of the present, see Baker and Palmer, *Early Modern Criticism in a Time of Crisis*
[193] www.macmorris.maynoothuniversity.ie/site/125.

'westward enterprise'[194] – advertises its 'Commodities' and the potential for colonists to turn anything they can lay their hands on into 'chaffare':

> Hides, and fish, Salmon, Hake, Herringe,
> Irish wooll, and linen cloth, faldinge,
> And [pine] marterns goode ben her marchandie.[195]

Robert Payne, sent as a prospector by investors sounding out opportunities in the Munster Plantation, reports equally enthusiastically on its 'commodities':

> There is two very riche countries called Kennory and Conelogh, both within the countie of Lemereck: they are called the gardens of the land for ye varietie and great plentie of all graine and fruites, and also there is more plentie of venison, fish and fowle then els where in Ireland, although in euery place there is great store.[196]

Empiricism and new scientific technologies provided the intellectual and practical instruments for marketising land. In 1586, in preparation for the Plantation of Munster, commissioners surveyed the late Earl of Desmond's attainted lands. In England, the new science of surveying was inseparable from the emergence of agrarian capitalism.[197] Transplanted to Munster in the wake of a devastating war, surveying emerged as a specialist arm of colonial mapmaking. Plantation surveys became not just instruments for alienating land from native landholders. They also framed that confiscated land within a new economic system which alienated (in a much more profound sense of the word) human actors from the more-than-human world. The Desmond Survey illustrates the process by which 'woods' (mentioned 596 times) were redescribed as 'timber' (mentioned 243 times), and goshawks, fish ponds, orchards and gardens, rivers rich in eels and salmon were all caught up in the wholesale conversion of customary exchanges (e.g. 'Tithes of fish')[198] into monetary – or, as Karl Polanyi would see it, 'fictitious' – valuations. The economic model of a pre-capitalist society, where redistribution and reciprocation governed social relations,[199] was being translated into one where everything had its price, in shillings, pennies, and white groats: 'xlv s iiij d ij w.g'.[200] When, at Lough Gur, the Desmond surveyors note that 'the castle and mountain

---

[194] See for example Andrews, Canny, Hair eds., *Westward Enterprise*.
[195] www.macmorris.maynoothuniversity.ie/site/22.
[196] www.macmorris.maynoothuniversity.ie/site/79.
[197] McRae, 'To Know One's Own', 333–57.
[198] www.macmorris.maynoothuniversity.ie/site/41, www.macmorris.maynoothuniversity.ie/site/76, www.macmorris.maynoothuniversity.ie/site/42; 'Tithes of fish' are mentioned just below the passage excerpted.
[199] Comninel, 'English Feudalism and the Origins of Capitalism', 1–53; Polanyi, *The Great Transformation*, p.84.
[200] www.macmorris.maynoothuniversity.ie/site/132.

shut in a fishery otherwise called a lough, full of river fish',[201] we have moved definitively into a world where we cannot see the wood for the lumber, or the lake for the commercial fishery. The process fits with Jason Moore's argument that 'the birth of Nature' was an 'ontological formation and world-praxis' perfected in colonial contexts: 'the rise of capitalism in the long sixteenth century was premised on a fundamentally new law of environment-making. Capitalism's "law of value" was, it turns out, a law of Cheap Nature.'[202] What we see being played out in early modern Ireland is the mobilisation of a new empirical epistemology and the commodification of the natural world in a process which Mauro Scalercio calls 'imperiality'. Scalercio defines imperiality as 'the power that humanity exerts over nature'. Imperiality is inherently expansionist and it moves in lockstep with colonialism, that 'peculiar form of action inspired by knowledge'.[203]

But of course, Ireland was not just a laboratory for proto-capitalism and the emerging discourses of the Capitalocene. Contiguous to the planters, prospectors, and surveyors were the keepers of very different kinds of knowledge. The value of juxtapuntal reading is that it allows us to push back against the instrumental knowledges of colonialism and counter them with more relational understandings of humans' enmeshment in a more-than-human world. 'As an epistemology and as a practice', Margaret Ramírez reminds us, 'the decolonial resists and rewrites colonial conceptions of land and embodiment. If colonialism denotes the conquest of land and the dispossession and erasure of Indigenous peoples, then to decolonize is to reconnect and reembody the relationship to land'.[204] Alongside the empiricism of the colonists lay a very different scale of measurement, where land could be valued for being 'éanamhuil', 'abundant in birds'.[205] It is, as the seventh extract at Dunboy (otherwise site of some of the cruellest and bloodiest accounts on the deep map) illustrates, a place where close observation opens a path to sympathy and reflection. Here is Pilib Ó Súilleabháin Béirre's description of the robin, from his *Historiae catholicae Iberniae compendium*:

> L. Sylvia, rubecula, G. ἐρίθακος, H. Camachuelo, I. Spideog bruin muintiri: corpore parvo, misercordia magna Ibernis in honoresummo habetur, quod hominum examina, desertaque cadavera musco, et herbis officiosa, et pia tergere conatur. Quamobrem ea invalet consuetudo, ut eam Iberni non occident, et quamvis canor sit, non petant in caveam, non capiant, quin etiam captam redimant, asserant in libertatem, atque dimittant;

---

[201] www.macmorris.maynoothuniversity.ie/site/43.
[202] Moore, 'The Rise of Cheap Nature', 78–115, 89, 91.
[203] Scalercio, 'Dominating Nature and Colonialism', 1076–1091, 1079, 1084.
[204] Naylor et al., 'Interventions', 205–206.
[205] www.macmorris.maynoothuniversity.ie/site/61.

> Small in body, it is held in the highest sympathy among the Irish because, pious and courteous, it tries to cover lifeless bodies and deserted corpses of men with moss and grass. For this reason, custom prevails that the Irish do not kill it and although it may be sweet sounding they do not seek it for a cage, nor do they capture it but even when it has been captured they redeem it, and they give it liberty and set it free.[206]

It is also a place where the poet Aonghus Ó Dálaigh Fionn can write a religious lyric infused with a sense of the natural world as integrated, harmonious, and rapturous:

> Moladh an ghaoth Rígh na reann
> moladh gach síon ní saoth liom
> do ní ealbha is foghar tonn
> moladh don donn fheardha fhionn.
>
> Molaid na héisg san mhuir mhór
> molaid guil éasga agus úr;

> May the wind praise the King of the stars! May all weathers praise Him! This is my joy! The flocks and the noisy waves praise the great bright Ruler!
>
> May the fish in the great sea, the heat, the moon and the earth praise Him!

One imperative for assembling a multilingual digital application rests on the belief that the archives of cultures minoritised by 'imperiality' are storehouses of alternative ways of being in the world. We know that global linguistic diversity constitutes an intellectual web of life or 'logosphere', where each language encodes a particular relationship with the ecosystem it most intimately knows.[207] Similarly, Irish-language texts which, at once, articulated long-sanctioned understandings of the natural world and resisted an alien incursion powered by a new extractive logic offer unique perspectives on that relationship. Now, amid the twin crises of climate breakdown and the sixth extinction, insights into how people interacted with the natural world prior to the emerging discourses of the Capitalocene allow us to access human imaginings of animate and responsive ontologies beyond the human which can replenish our ecological imaginary.

To explore where comparative, multilingual, decolonial, eco-critical readings may take us, let's start at Bantry. The map pin there brings us to three extracts. In the first, Edmund Spenser recommends the garrisoning of the town and the exploitation of its 'plentifull fishinge'.[208] In the third, Richard Beacon declares

---

[206] www.macmorris.maynoothuniversity.ie/site/191.
[207] See, for example, Krauss 'The World's Languages in Crisis', 4–10; Suckling, 'A House on Fire', 193–202.
[208] www.macmorris.maynoothuniversity.ie/site/81.

Ireland to be 'a common-wealth overgrowne with a generall corruption of manners, and thereby become savage, barbarous, and barren'. But Beacon has the solution: 'like vnto the wilde olive and figge tree [Ireland] may by the continuall pruning and addressing of a skilfull magistrate, be made obedient, civill, and profitable'. In using pollarding as a metaphor for imposing 'sharpe correction and discipline', Beacon indicates that, if the colony is to be made 'profitable', controlling the natives and controlling nature amounts to the same thing.[209] In the new colonial order of enclosure and extraction, both will 'be made obedient ... and profitable'. In between the two colonial extracts comes Tadhg Ó Dálaigh's elegy for Eóghan Óg Ó Súilleabháin which brings us to a very different ecological dispensation:

> Do bhí meidhe na muire
> do bhí an talamh toghuidhe
> bárr na sgath, donnghrán na ndreas
> comhlán do rath 'na réimeas.
>
> Robudh suaimhneach na sreabha
> fa háluinn na hairgheadha
> fá corcra ceannbhrat na néall
> do deaghmhac ochta Oilean.
>
> An ionbhuigh bá fear faire
> d'iath Bearra agus Beanntraighe
> ar feadh na ccríoch bhfonnbhláth bhfionn
> bá comhghnáth síoth is soinionn. (31–33)

The promontory, the best of the land, the blossoms of flower heads, the golden fruits of the thorn-bushes, were all absolutely filled with prosperity during his reign.

The streams were peaceful, the cattle herds were splendid, the covering cloak of the clouds was purple, because of the good son of the bosom of Oiléan.

While he was watchman of the land of Beare and Bantry, peace and cheerfulness was the norm across the land white with flowers.[210]

For the Gaelic poets, the quality of a ruler is revealed by the well-being of the natural world. Whereas for Beacon, the 'prince' oversees the disciplining of both native and nature, in the bardic tradition, good governance is confirmed by the flourishing of the natural world. In his inauguration ode for Donnchadh Ó Briain, 4th Earl of Thomond, the poet, Tadhg Mac Bruaideadha, anticipates an intensified natural exuberance, responsive to the new lord's qualities:

---

[209] www.macmorris.maynoothuniversity.ie/site/199.
[210] www.macmorris.maynoothuniversity.ie/site/12.

> Biaidh dord beach ós barraibh fiodh
> biaidh luth breac ar fud inbhear
> god chomhmoladh ag cur leam
> is tromfhogur dhamh ndíleann;

> There will be buzzing of bees above the tops of woods, movement of trout throughout the estuaries, and heavy lowing of great oxen joining in my praise of you.[211]

The belief that 'the proper functioning of nature is a consequence of the just and wise ruler' was deeply rooted in Irish culture. One of the earliest texts of Old Irish gnomic literature, *Audacht Morainn*, insisted that the 'justice of the ruler' (*fír flathemon*) and the well-being of nature were inseparable and interdependent:

> It is through the justice of the ruler (*Is tre fír flathemon*) that abundances of great tree-fruit of the great wood are tasted. It is through the justice of the ruler that milk-yields of great cattle are maintained. It is through the justice of the ruler that there is abundance of every high, tall corn. It is through the justice of the ruler that abundance of fish swim in streams.[212]

So much flowed from this fundamental belief: the residual conceit that the ruler entered into a sacral (or metaphorical) marriage with the land, seen when Domhnall Mac Carthaigh is described as the 'spouse', 'céile', of his territory;[213] or the quasi-shamanic reference to three Ó Briain princes as

> na trí bhile buantoraidh ...
> Trí seabhaic go séan seilge ...
> Trí beithreacha go mbuaidh gliadh ...
> trí sgealláin ubhaill óirchnis ...
> Trí húrchna is uaisle mogail,trí sreabha a haill fhíorthobair;

> three venerable trees ever fruitful ...
> Three hawks fortunate in the chase ...
> Three bears victorious in fight ...
> three pips of a gold-skinned apple
> Three fresh hazelnuts from the finest cluster, three streams
> from the rock of a clear spring.[214]

That the mark of leadership is a connection to the natural world and that the bond between the ruler and the natural world is mutually sustaining now seem less like an archaism than an idea whose time has – or needs to – come (back).

---

[211] www.macmorris.maynoothuniversity.ie/site/154.
[212] Maier, 'Sacral Kingship in Pre-Christian Ireland', 12–32, 16; Maier quotes Fergus Kelly's edition and translation of *Audacht Morainn* on page 20.
[213] www.macmorris.maynoothuniversity.ie/site/28.
[214] www.macmorris.maynoothuniversity.ie/site/113. On residual animism in bardic poetry, see Palmer, 'Coda'.

This connection between the past (the extracts) and the present (the moment of reading) encapsulates the twin-temporality of decolonisation. Understandings of the natural world which had to be excluded in early modernity in order for colonisation/coloniality to thrive, then and now, speak very differently amid the policrises of the present. Here again, the deep map is reconfiguring our engagement with temporality. In Section 3, we saw how the freeze-frame effect of spatialising texts worked against teleology. Now, we see that it also works against a rigid separation of the past from the present. Raymond Williams' concept of 'emergent', 'residual', and 'archaic' discourses, and his demonstration that all three coexist simultaneously, helps to explain why the flux of ideas isn't univalent or teleological: 'emergent' discourses (the discourses of proto-capitalism and the Anthropocene, in the case of the deep map) don't have the field all to themselves. 'The residual', Williams reminds us, 'has been effectively formed in the past, but is still active ... not at all as an element of the past, but as an effective element of the present ... [which] may have an alternative or even oppositional relation to the dominant culture'. Even the 'archaic' which Williams defines as 'that which is wholly recognised as an element of the past'[215] may still open up possibilities in the present. Those are the possibilities opened up by juxtapuntal decolonial reading.

5 Coda

Every once in a while, little details make their way onto colonial maps which seem to exceed their frameworks of utility or explanation. Two such instances on John Speed's 'Province of Munster' (our historical map layer) allow us to reflect on what it means to move from a colonial map to a deep map. The first is a string of italicised lettering splayed across the River Feale and onto the hillock icons denoting the Stack's Mountains: '*I. McDonell Rymer*'. One task for the MACMORRIS team when seeking to recover perspectives occluded by colonisation was to trace writers and other cultural producers who had slipped out of history. For most, nothing survives but a name. Many of these names were recovered from the *Fiants*, which recorded pardons granted to those who had 'rebelled' against the Crown. Just to the north-west of '*I. McDonell Rymer*', for example, a map pin brings us to the 'Pardon to Nich. Dall, of Ratoo, harper'. The accompanying image, taken from a gorgeously decorated copy of Speed's map, features a red-cheeked harper astride a monstrous flying fish which is surfing westwards across Tralee Bay.[216] Of the music 'blind Nicholas' played, however, not a note survives. Almost always, the names

---

[215] Williams, *Marxism and Literature*, pp.121–22.
[216] Speed, 'Province of Mounster, with the City of Cork'.

recovered in sources like the *Fiants* come without text or story. We get a precious sighting of a woman poet – 'Mary-ny-Donoghue, a she-barde' – but not a line of her poetry.[217] (Indeed, to include any woman poet on the deep map we had to bend our inclusion criteria, in line with a feminist data ethic, beyond the cut-off date of 1610; Fionnuala Uí Bhriain scrapes in with a poem dating from 1617.)[218]

As for 'I. McDonell Rymer', we found no further trace of him. His presence, stretched across the map from the Cashen River to Sliabh Luachra, is just as arresting as is his absolute absence in all other sources. In that mixture of presence and absence, this silent poet speaks for the deep map too. The oddity of his inscription onto the landscape is an almost chthonic assertion of what, at every other level, the colonial map sought to erase. McDonell's presence, writ large on the landscape, is a reminder, too, that those, like him, who were rooted in an intimately known and storied world had no need of maps. As Amy Mulligan points out, 'Ireland lacks the great *mappae mundi*, but its poets map the same scheme in words: Irish landscapes are verbal rather than visual.' The Irish poetics of place is underpinned by the metrical *Dindseanchas*, the onomastic 'lore of place' which professional poets or *filidh* learnt as part of their bardic-school training. '[P]lace-making poets' were 'Ireland's geographers', creating 'a national landscape, a virtual Ireland':

> Ireland did not participate in the production of elaborate cartographies. Rather, it was the class of poets who staked out the role of Ireland's mapmakers, with medieval Irish geography becoming a verbal undertaking rather than a cartographic one.

Colonial cartography is, Mulligan concludes, 'the inverse of the native poetics of place'.[219]

Sometimes, 'home' is a place of meaning so intense that its celebration radiates an almost Heideggerian sense of 'dwelling'. So it is when Seaán Ó Maoil Chonaire comes back to his family's school of history and genealogy in Ard Choill:

> seanadhba nach cóir do choill
> róimh na healadhna an Ardchoill ...
>
> Críoch easach innseach [fh]éarach
> críoch chruithgheal chaomh chaisleánach;
> críoch shéadach fholtach fhuilteach
> torthach tréadach thiodhlaicdheach;

---

[217] www.macmorris.maynoothuniversity.ie/profile/m5720.
[218] www.macmorris.maynoothuniversity.ie/site/31; Bourke, 'Networking Early Modern Irish Women', 270–85.
[219] Mulligan, *A Landscape of Words*, p.7, p.18, p.109, p.178.

> Ardchoill – that Rome of the arts –
> an old abode that should not be violated.
>
> The grassy district of waterfalls, and islands,
> the bright, pleasant shapely district abundant in castles,
> the ridged district of treasures and wealth,
> fruitful, abounding in flocks and gifts.[220]

But elsewhere on the map, there are intimations of change, hints of a culture becoming unhoused. In his elegy for Domhnall Mac Carthaigh Mór, Aonghus Ó Dálaigh Fionn laments that he can no longer hear the accents of the Gael – 'gan ghuth aoinfhir d'fhuil Gaoidheal' – in the ancient capital of Cashel.[221] One poet bitterly intrudes English words into an Irish-language poem as indices of a wider contamination:

> Drong do *sheduction* lándo chuir *corruption* sa choir;
>
> A group of 'seduction' through and through, who 'corrupted' righteousness.[222]

Another finds that there is nobody left to value his high art:

> Gé dán sin go snadhmadh bhfis,
> gach margadh ó chrois go crois
> do shiobhail mé an Mhumhain leis -
> ní breis é a-nuraidh ná a-nois;
>
> Though this is a poem with close-knit science, I have walked all Munster with it, every market from cross to cross – nothing gained from last year to this time.[223]

'*I. McDonell Rymer*', therefore, is a complex emblem for the deep map. It insists on presence while marking an absence. In that, it represents a silent call that the deep map answers, to reinscribe on the colonial map the very things it sought to exclude and was instrumental in extinguishing.

The second case where a detail on the map projects meanings beyond the boundaries of Speed's cartographic universe is the 'Speaking Stone', east of Dungarvan. *Cloch Labhrais*, the 'speaking' or 'answering' stone, is a glacial erratic capable, according to legend, of responding to perjuries uttered in its presence. The excess of meaning here is partly cultural; it leads us outward into stories and world views encoded in *seanchas*. But much more pressingly, the boundary breaching performed by the 'Speaking Stone' is temporal.

---

[220] www.macmorris.maynoothuniversity.ie/site/40.
[221] www.macmorris.maynoothuniversity.ie/site/28.
[222] www.macmorris.maynoothuniversity.ie/site/137: Our italics.
[223] www.macmorris.maynoothuniversity.ie/site/135.

A conglomerate rock formed at the end of a glacial period from even older deposits, the 'Speaking Stone' projects us into deep time – as, when we think about it, all the topographical features on the map have the capacity to do.

Time, as we have been seeing, keeps forcing its way onto the deep map. There is no escaping the fact that the encounter that it captures aslant is, ineluctably, a story of conquest, colonisation, and loss. Ultimately, Ardchoill, the 'old abode that should not be violated', *will* be; the poems of Mary-ny-Donoghue, the 'she-barde', will be lost. The life and works of I. McDonell Rymer will be winnowed down to italic lettering on the map of a conquered province. But none of that happens here. Section 3 showed how the freeze-frame effect of deep mapping works against colonial teleology. Section 4 indicated that ideas seemingly interred in the past have, when exhumed, a way of speaking to the present. In that sense, the deep map participates in Walter Benjamin's rejection of a teleological model of history that, in recording 'the triumphal procession' of the victors, offers no court of appeal to the defeated and the oppressed. A central tenet behind the deep map is that ideas forced out of history by colonial proto-modernity can, when reintroduced to the present, resonate anew. In that, the deep map operates in a similar time zone to that invoked by Benjamin when he says that '[h]istory is the subject of a construction whose site is not homogenous, empty time, but … a past charged with now-time [*Jetztzeit*], a past … blasted out of the continuum of history.'[224] But the 'Speaking Stone' of West Waterford opens up yet another temporal dimension – deep time – and, with it, ontologies beyond the human. It opens up the temporality signalled by Dipesh Chakrabarty when he says that '[a]nthropogenic explanations of climate change spell the collapse of the age-old humanist distinction between natural history and human history'.[225] That deeper perspective reminds us that the project of decolonising needs to move beyond languages and cultures, to address the colonisation of the earth itself. 'By divesting our capitalist modernity of its status as the naturally ordained telos of our species story', Greg Anderson argues, 'an ontological turn in our practice would raise the possibility of a new strain of critical theory, something like a non-modern critique of the modern'.[226] If the deep map is, among many other things, about deep time, it is also, most urgently, about the present.

---

[224] Benjamin, 'On the Concept of History', Thesis VII: 47, Thesis XIV: 86.
[225] Chakrabarty, 'The Climate of History', 197–222, 201.
[226] Anderson, *The Realness of Things Past*, pp.254–55.

Bibliography

Manuscript Sources

Cecil, William. '17 June 1586, Extracted Maps and Plans', TNA MPF 1/273.

Goghe, John. 'Hibernia: Insula non procul ab Anglia vulgare Hirlandia vocata', TNA MPF 1/68.

Jobson, Francis. 'The Province of Munster', IE TCD MS 1209/36.

Jobson, Francis. 'The Province of Munster', P/49(20); MS 53–073.

Lythe, Robert. 'Munster. "A Single draght of Mounster": Map showing place-names, rivers, mountains, names of Irish nobility and chieftains. Scale: 1 inch to 5 Irish miles. Compass star. [? Drawn by Robert Lythe]. Additions in hand of Lord Burghley. in hand of Lord Burghley', TNA MPF 1/73.

Perry-Castañeda Library Map Collection, University of Texas at Austin, Map No. 504014 1979.

Speed, John. 'Province of Mounster, with the City of Cork', IE TCD MS 1209/38.

Printed Sources

Amrith, Sunil. *The Burning Earth: A History* (London: Norton, 2024).

Anderson, Greg. *The Realness of Things Past: Ancient Greece and Ontological History* (Oxford: Oxford University Press, 2018).

Andrews, John Harwood. 'The Irish Surveys of Robert Lythe', *Imago Mundi* 19.1 (1965), 22–31.

Andrews, Kenneth R., Nicholas P. Canny, and Paul Edward Hedley Hair, eds. *Westward Enterprise: English Activities in Ireland, the Atlantic, and America, 1480–1650* (Detroit, MI: Wayne State University Press, 1979).

Baker, David, and Patricia Palmer. *Early Modern Criticism in a Time of Crisis* (Santa Barbara, CA: University of California Santa Barbara: emcIMPRINT, 2022): www.emctc.tome.press/.

Bakhtin, Mikhail M. 'Forms of Time and of the Chronotope in the Novel: Notes toward a Historical Poetics'. In Michael Holquist, ed. *The Dialogic Imagination: Four Essays* (Austin, TX: University of Texas Press, 2020), pp. 84–259.

Bassnett, Susan. 'Reflections on Comparative Literature in the Twenty-First Century', *Comparative Critical Studies* 3.1–2 (2006), 3–11.

Bauch, Nicholas. 'Designing for Mysterious Encounter: Three Scales of Integration in Deep Mapmaking'. In David J. Bodenhamer, John Corrigan, and Trevor M. Harris, eds. *Making Deep Maps: Foundations, Approaches, and Methods* (London: Routledge, 2022), pp.38–50.

Benjamin, Walter. 'On the Concept of History'. In Michael Löwy, ed. *Fire Alarm: Reading Walter Benjamin's 'On the Concept of History'*, trans. Chris Turner (London: Verso, 2016).

Bhandar, Brenna. *Colonial Lives of Property: Law, Land and Racial Regimes of Ownership* (Durham, NC: Duke University Press, 2018).

Blomley, Nicholas. 'Uncritical Critical Geography?' *Progress in Human Geography* 30.1 (2006), 87–94.

Boatcă, Manuela. 'Counter-Mapping as Method', *Historical Social Research / Historische Sozialforschung, Special Issue: Reflexivity between Science and Society* 46.2 (2021), 244–63.

Bodenhamer, David. 'Narrating Space and Place'. In David J. Bodenhamer, John Corrigan, and Trevor M. Harris, eds., *Deep Maps and Spatial Narratives* (Bloomington, IN: Indiana University Press, 2015), pp.7–27.

Bodenhamer, David J. 'The Varieties of Deep Maps'. In David J. Bodenhamer, John Corrigan, and Trevor M. Harris, eds. *Making Deep Maps: Foundations, Approaches, and Methods* (London: Routledge, 2022), pp.1–16.

Bodenhamer, David J., John Corrigan, and Trevor M. Harris, eds. *Deep Maps and Spatial Narratives* (Bloomington, IN: Indiana University Press, 2015).

Bodenhamer, David J., John Corrigan, and Trevor M. Harris, 'Introduction'. In David J. Bodenhamer, John Corrigan, and Trevor M. Harris, eds., *Deep Maps and Spatial Narratives* (Bloomington, IN: Indiana University Press, 2015), pp. 1–7.

Bodenhamer, David J., John Corrigan, and Trevor M. Harris, eds. *Making Deep Maps: Foundations, Approaches, and Methods* (London: Routledge, 2022).

Bodenhamer, David J., John Corrigan, and Trevor M. Harris, 'Preface'. In David J. Bodenhamer, John Corrigan, and Trevor M. Harris, eds. *Making Deep Maps: Foundations, Approaches, and Methods* (London: Routledge, 2022), pp. xiii–xvi.

Bourke, Evan. 'Networking Early Modern Irish Women', *Irish Historical Studies* 46.170 (2022), 270–85.

Bourke, Evan. 'Deep Mapping Spenser in Munster'. In Evan Bourke, Deirdre Nic Chárthaigh, and Philip Mac a' Ghoill, eds. *Spenser and the Filidh in Early Modern Ireland* (Suffolk: Boydell and Brewer, Forthcoming).

Bradshaw, Brendan. *'And so Began the Irish Nation': Nationality, National Consciousness and Nationalism in Pre-modern Ireland* (London: Ashgate, 2015).

Bradshaw, Brendan. 'Nationalism and Historical Scholarship in Modern Ireland.' *Irish Historical Studies* 26.104 (November 1989), 329–51.

Breen, John. 'The Empirical Eye: Edmund Spenser's *A View of the Present State of Ireland*', *The Irish Review* 16 (1994), 44–52.

Brindle, Stephen. *Architecture in Britain and Ireland: 1530–1830* (London: Paul Mellon, 2023).

Burlinson, Christopher. *Allegory, Space, and the Material World in the Writings of Edmund Spenser* (Cambridge: Cambridge University Press, 2006).

Canny, Nicholas. *The Elizabethan Conquest of Ireland: A Pattern Established 1565–1576* (Hassocks: Harvester Press, 1976).

Carey, Vincent P. 'Atrocity and History: Grey, Spenser and the Slaughter at Smerwick (1580)'. In David Edwards, Pádraig Lenihan, and Clodagh Tait, eds. *Age of Atrocity: Violence and Political Conflict in Early Modern Ireland* (Dublin: Four Courts, 2007), pp.79–94.

Carpenter, Andrew. *Verse in English from Tudor and Stuart Ireland* (Cork: Cork University Press, 2004).

Carr, Edward H. *What Is History?* (London: Penguin, 1964).

Chakrabarty, Dipesh. 'The Climate of History: Four Theses', *Critical Inquiry* 35.2 (2009), 197–222.

Cohn, Bernard. *Colonialism and Its Forms of Knowledge: The British in India* (Princeton, NJ: Princeton University Press, 1996).

Comninel, George C. 'English Feudalism and the Origins of Capitalism', *The Journal of Peasant Studies* 27.4 (2000), 1–53.

Coughlan, Patricia. *Spenser and Ireland: An Interdisciplinary Approach* (Cork: Cork University Press, 1989).

Crampton, Jeremy W. *Mapping: A Critical Introduction to Cartography and GIS* (Blackwell, OK: John Wiley & Sons, 2010).

Cresswell, Tim. *Place: An Introduction* (Newark: John Wiley & Sons, 2014).

Cronin, Michael. *An Ghaeilge agus An Éirceolaíocht – Irish and Ecology* (BÁC: Foilseacháin Ábhair Spioradálta, 2019).

Dalton, Craig and Liz Mason-Deese. 'Counter (Mapping) Actions: Mapping as Militant Research', *ACME* 11.3 (2012), 439–66.

Dalton, Craig M. and Tim Stallmann. 'Counter-Mapping Data Science', *The Canadian Geographer / Le Geographe canadien* 62.1 (2018), 93–101.

Damrosch, David. *Comparing the Literatures: Literary Studies in a Global Age* (Princeton, NJ: Princeton University Press, 2022).

De Fréine, Seán. *The Great Silence: The Study of a Relationship between Language and Nationality* (Cork: Mercier Press, 1978).

Delanda, Manuel. *A New Philosophy of Society* (London: Continuum, 2006).

Deleuze Gilles, and Felix Guattari. *A Thousand Plateaus: Capitalism and Schizophrenia*, trans. Brian Massumi (Minneapolis, MN: University of Minnesota Press, 1987).

Derrida, Jacques. 'Archive Fever: A Freudian Impression', trans. Eric Prenowitz, *Diacritics* 25.2 (1995), 9–63.
Dovey, Kim. *Becoming Places: Urbanism/Architecture/Identity/Power* (Abingdon: Routledge, 2010).
Dussel, Enrique. *The Underside of Modernity* (Atlantic Highlands, NJ: Humanities Press, 1996).
Edwards, David, Pádraig Lenihan, and Clodagh Tait, eds., *Age of Atrocity: Violence and Political Conflict in Early Modern Ireland* (Dublin: Four Courts, 2007).
Escobar, Arturo. 'Worlds and Knowledges Otherwise: The Latin American Modernity/Coloniality Research Program', *Cultural Studies* 21.2–3 (2007), 179–210.
Fabian, Johannes. *Time and the Other: How Anthropology Makes Its Object* (New York: Columbia University Press, 2014).
Fanon, Frantz. *The Wretched of the Earth* (New York: Grove Press, 1963).
Fisher Fishkin, Shelley. '"Deep Maps": A Brief for Digital Palimpsest Mapping Projects (DPMPs, or "Deep Maps")', *Journal of Transnational American Studies* 3.2(2011), 1–31.
Friel, Brian. *Translations* (London: Faber, 1981).
Fritzsche, K. Peter. 'Unable to be Tolerant?' In Russell F. Farnen, Karl Peter Fritzsche, Ivan Kos, and Riidiger Meyenberg, eds. *Tolerance in Transition* (Oldenburg: Bibliotheks und Informationssystem der Universitat Oldenburg, 2001), pp.1–9.
Gainsford, Thomas. *The True Exemplary, and Remarkable History of the Earle of Tirone* (London, 1619).
Ghosh, Amitav. *The Nutmeg's Curse: Parables for a Planet in Crisis* (Chicago, IL: University of Chicago Press, 2021).
Hadfield, Andrew. *Spenser's Irish Experience: Wilde Fruit and Salvage Soil* (Oxford: Oxford University Press, 1997).
HadžiMuhamedović, Safet. *Waiting for Elijah: Time and Encounter in a Bosnian Landscape* (New York: Berghahn Books, 2018).
Harley, John Brian. *History of Cartography. Vol. 1.* (Chicago, IL: University of Chicago Press, 1992).
Harris, Jason, ed. *Making Ireland Roman: Irish Neo-Latin Writers and the Republic of Letters* (Cork: Cork University Press, 2009).
Harris, Leila M., and Helen D. Hazen. 'The Power of Maps: (Counter) Mapping for Conservation', *ACME: An International E-Journal for Critical Geographies* 4.1 (2005), 99–130.
Hartley, John Brian. 'Deconstructing the Map', *Cartographica* 26.2 (1989), 1–20.

Hartley, John Brian. 'Silences and Secrecy: The Hidden Agenda of Cartography in Early Modern Europe', *Imago Mundi* 40 (1988), 57–76.

Hartman, Saidiya. 'Venus in Two Acts', *Small Axe* 26, 12.2 (June 2008), 1–14.

Heaney, Seamus. *North* (London: Faber and Faber, 1975).

Heaney, Seamus. 'Ocean's Love to Ireland'. In *North* (London: Faber and Faber, 1975), p. 40.

Herron, Thomas. *Spenser's Irish Work: Poetry, Plantation and Colonial Reformation* (Aldershot: Ashgate, 2007).

Humphris, Imogen, Lummina G. Horlings, and Iain Biggs, '"Getting Deep into Things": Deep Mapping in a "Vacant" Landscape'. In Alex Franklin, ed. *Co-Creativity and Engaged Scholarship* (London: Palgrave, 2022), pp.357–90.

Hunt, Dallas and Shaun A. Stevenson. 'Decolonizing Geographies of Power: Indigenous Digital Counter-Mapping Practices on Turtle Island', *Settler Colonial Studies* 7.3 (2016), 372–92.

Kane, Brendan and Patrick Wadden eds., *An Eoraip: Gaelic Ireland in Medieval and Early Modern Europe* (Leiden: Brill, 2025).

Kane, Brendan, 'Keith Sidwell and David Edwards, eds. "The Tipperary Hero: Dermot O'Meara's *Ormonius* (1615)"'. *Spenser Review* 44.2.46 (Fall 2014). http://www.english.cam.ac.uk/spenseronline/review/volume-44/442/reviews/sidwell-keith-and-david-edwards-eds-the-tipperary-hero-dermot-omearas-ormonius-1.

Kelsall, Malcolm. *Literary Representations of the Irish Country House: Civilisation and Savagery under the Union* (Hampshire: Palgrave Macmillan, 2003).

Kirschenbaum, Matthew. 'Hello Worlds,' *Chronicle of Higher Education*, 23 January 2009, www.chronicle.com/article/Hello-Worlds/5476.

Klein, Bernhard. *Maps and the Writing of Space in Early Modern England and Ireland* (Basingstoke: Palgrave, 2001).

Krauss, Michael. 'The World's Languages in Crisis', *Language* 68 (1992), 4–10.

Latour, Bruno. *We Have Never Been Modern*, trans. Catherine Porter (Cambridge, MA: Harvard University Press, 1993).

Lewis, Simon L. and Mark A. Maslin. *The Human Planet: How We Created the Anthropocene* (London: Pelican, 2018).

Løgstrup, Joanne. *The Contemporary Condition: Coexistence of Times – A Conversation with John Akomfrah* (Berlin: Sternberg Press, 2020).

Maier, Bernhard. 'Sacral Kingship in Pre-Christian Ireland', *Zeitschrift für Religions- und Geistesgeschichte* 41.1 (1989), 12–32.

Maley, Willy. *Salvaging Spenser: Colonialism, Culture and Identity* (Basingstoke: Palgrave, 1997).

Marx, Karl and Engels, Frederick. *Marx and Engels on Ireland* (London: Lawrence & Wishart, 1971).

McCloskey, James. *Voices Silenced: Has Irish a Future? / Guthanna in Ëag: An Mairfidh an Ghaeilge Beo?* (Dublin: Cois Life Teoranta, 2001).

Mc Manus, Damian, and Eoin Ó Raghallaigh, eds., *A Bardic Miscellany: Five Hundred Bardic Poems from Manuscripts in Irish and British Libraries* (Dublin: Trinity College Dublin, 2010).

McRae, Andrew. 'To Know One's Own: Estate Surveying and the Representation of the Land in Early Modern England', *Huntington Library Quarterly* 56.4 (Autumn, 1993), 333–57.

Mignolo, Walter D. 'Foreword: On Pluriversality and Multipolarity'. In Bernd Reiterx, ed. *Constructing the Pluriverse: The Geopolitics of Knowledge* (Durham, NC: Duke University Press, 2018), i–xii.

Mignolo, Walter D. 'Introduction: Coloniality of Power and De-Colonial Thinking', *Cultural Studies* 21.2–3 (2007), 155–56.

Mignolo, Walter D. *Local Histories/Global Designs: Coloniality, Subaltern Knowledges, and Border Thinking* (Princeton, NJ: Princeton University Press, 2012).

Mignolo, Walter D. *The Darker Side of the Renaissance: Literacy, Territoriality, and Colonization* (Ann Arbor, MI: University of Michigan Press, 1995).

Miller, Carolyn R. 'Forword'. In Phillip Sipiora and James S. Baumlin, eds. *Rhetoric and Kairos: Essays in History, Theory and Praxis* (New York: John Hopkins Press, 2002), pp. xi–xiii.

Montagu, Basil. *The Works of Francis Bacon*, 16 vols. (London: William Pickering, 1825–1834).

Montague, John. 'A Lost Tradition', Section IV, A Severed Head. In *The Rough Field* (Oldcastle: Gallery Press, 1972), pp. 37–39.

Montaño, John Patrick. *The Roots of English Colonialism in Ireland* (Cambridge: Cambridge University Press, 2012).

Moore, Jason. 'The Rise of Cheap Nature'. In Jason Moore, ed. *Anthropocene or Capitalocene?: Nature, History, and the Crisis of Capitalism* (Oakland, CA: PM Press, 2016), pp.78–115.

Morrin, James, ed. *Calendar of the Patent and Close Rolls of Chancery of Ireland* (Dublin: Thom, 1861–62).

Moryson, Fynes. *The Commonwealth of Ireland*, trans., Charles Hughes, p. 289. https://celt.ucc.ie/published/T100072/text001.html.

Mulligan, Amy C. *A Landscape of Words: Ireland, Britain and the Poetics of Space, 700–1250* (Manchester: Manchester University Press, 2019).

Naylor, Lindsay, Michelle Daigle, Sofia Zaragocin, Margaret Marietta Ramírez, and Mary Gilmartin. 'Interventions: Bringing the Decolonial to Political Geography', *Political Geography* 66 (2018), 199–209.

Nic Dháibhéid, Caoimhe, Shahmima Akhtar, Dónal Hassett et al. 'Round Table: Decolonising Irish History? Possibilities, Challenges, Practices'. *Irish Historical Studies* 45.168 (November 2021), 303–32.

O'Connor, Thomas. *Irish Voices from the Spanish Inquisition: Migrants, Converts and Brokers in Early Modern Iberia* (Basingstoke: Palgrave-Macmillan, 2016).

Ó Siochrú, Micheál and David Brown. 'The Down Survey and the Cromwellian Land Settlement'. In Jane Ohlmeyer, ed., *The Cambridge History of Ireland, 1550–1730* (Cambridge: Cambridge University Press, 2018), pp.584–607.

Oslender, Ulrich. 'Decolonizing Cartography and Ontological Conflict: Counter-Mapping in Colombia and "Cartographies Otherwise"', *Political Geography* 89 (2021), 1–12.

Ó Súilleabháin Béirre, Pilib. *Historiae Catholicae Iberniae Compendium* (Lisbon, 1621).

Palmer, Patricia. 'Another Past Was Possible: Mapping the Path from MACMORRIS to Port Harcourt'. In David Baker and Patricia Palmer, ed. *Early Modern Criticism and Politics in a Time of Crisis* (Santa Barbara, CA: EMC Imprint, 2022): https://emctc.tome.press/.

Palmer, Patricia. 'Coda: Animacy, the "Unthought", and a Poem to a Sacred Tree'. In David Baker and Patricia Palmer, eds. *Early Modern Criticism and Politics in a Time of Crisis* (Santa Barbara, CA: EMC Imprint, 2022): www.emctc.tome.press/chapter/coda-animacy-the-unthought-and-a-poem-to-a-sacred-tree/.

Palmer, Patricia. *Language and Conquest in Early Modern Ireland: English Renaissance Literature and Elizabethan Imperial Expansion* (Cambridge: Cambridge University Press, 2001).

Palmer, Patricia. *Making MACMORRIS: New Gleanings from Early Modern Ireland* (Maynooth: School of Celtic Studies, Maynooth University, 2024).

Palmer, Patricia. 'Missing Bodies, Absent Bards: Spenser, Shakespeare and a Crisis in Criticism', *English Literary Renaissance* 36.3 (Autumn 2006), 376–95.

Palmer, Patricia. 'The Gaelic Court and Country House Poetry: The Politics of an Overlooked Irish Genre'. In David Edwards and Brendan Kane, eds. *Tudor Ireland and Renaissance Court Society* (Manchester: Manchester University Press, 2024), pp.65–85.

Palmer, Patricia, David J. Baker, and Willy Maley. 'What Ish My Network? Introducing MACMORRIS: Digitising Cultural Activity and Collaborative

Networks in Early Modern Ireland', *Literature Compass* 15.11 (2018): https://doi.org/10.1111/lic3.12496.

Paul, Joanne. 'The Use of *Kairos* in Renaissance Political Philosophy', *Renaissance Quarterly* 67.1 (2014), 43–78.

Pearce, Margaret and Michael Hermann. 'Decolonizing Historical Cartography through Narrative: Champlain's Travels Revisited', paper presented to the Association of American Geographers, Boston, 2008.

Peluso, Nancy Lee. 'Whose Woods Are These?: Counter-Mapping Forest Territories in Kalimantan, Indonesia', *Antipode* 274 (1995), 383–406.

Polanyi, Karl. *The Great Transformation: The Political and Economic Origins of Our Time* (1944; London: Penguin, 2004).

Pratt, Mary Louise. 'Arts of the Contact Zone', *Profession* (1991), 33–40.

Quijano, Anibal. 'Coloniality of Power, Eurocentrism, and Latin America', *International Sociology* 15.2 (2000), 215–32.

Quiquivix, Linda. 'Art of War, Art of Resistance: Palestinian Counter-Cartography on Google Earth', *Annals of the Association of American Geographers* 104.3 (2014), 444–59.

Rancière, Jacques. *The Politics of Aesthetics*, trans. Gabriel Rockhill (London: Bloomsbury, 2013).

Risam, Roopika. 'Decolonizing the Digital Humanities in Theory and Practice'. In Jentery Sayers, ed. *The Routledge Companion to Media Studies and Digital Humanities* (London: Routledge, 2018), pp.78–86.

Risam, Roopika. *New Digital Worlds: Postcolonial Digital Humanities in Theory, Praxis, and Pedagogy* (Evanston, IL: Northwestern University Press, 2018).

Robertson, Stephen, and Lincoln A. Mullen. 'Navigating through Narrative'. In David J. Bodenhamer, John Corrigan, and Trevor M. Harris, eds. *Making Deep Maps: Foundations, Approaches, and Methods* (London: Routledge, 2022), pp.132–47.

Sack, Robert David. *Human Territoriality: Its Theory and History* (Cambridge: Cambridge University Press, 1986), p.48.

Said, Edward. *Culture and Imperialism* (New York: Vintage, 1993).

Scalercio, Mauro. 'Dominating Nature and Colonialism: Francis Bacon's View of Europe and the New World', *History of European Ideas* 44 (2018), 1076–1091.

Singh, Amardeep. 'Beyond the Archive Gap: The Kiplings and the Famines of British Colonial India', *South Asian Review* 40:3 (2019), 237–51.

Slomanson, Peter. 'On the Great Silence: A Gap in Irish Historiography and Consequences for Language Education in Ireland', *Nordic Irish Studies* 11.2 (2012), 95–114.

Smyth, William J. *Map-Making, Landscapes and Memory: A Geography of Colonial and Early Modern Ireland c. 1530–1750* (Cork: Cork University Press, 2006).

Speed, John. *The Invasions of England and Ireland with al Their Civill Wars since the Conquest* (London, 1667).

Spenser, Edmund. *A View of the Present State of Ireland*, eds. Andrew Hadfield and Willy Maley (Oxford: Blackwell, 1997).

Spivak, Gayatri Chakravorty. *Death of a Discipline* (New York: Columbia University Press, 2005).

Stradling, Robert. *Multiperspectivity in History Teaching: A Guide for Teachers* (Council of Europe, 2003).

Suckling, Kieran. 'A House on Fire: Connecting the Biological and Linguistic Diversity Crises', *Animal Law* 6 (2000), 193–202.

Tait, Clodagh, David Edwards, and Pádraig Lenihan. 'Early Modern Ireland: A History of Violence'. In David Edwards, Pádraig Lenihan, and Clodagh Tait, eds. *Age of Atrocity: Violence and Political Conflict in Early Modern Ireland* (Dublin: Four Courts, 2007), pp.14–15.

Teskey, Gordon. *Allegory and Violence* (Ithaca, NY: Cornell University Press, 1996).

The Statutes at Large Passed in the Parliaments Held in Ireland, vol. 1 (Dublin, 1786).

Travis, Charles. 'GIS and History: Epistemologies, Reflections, and Considerations'. In Alexander von Lünen and Charles Travis, eds. *History and GIS: Epistemologies, Considerations, and Reflections* (Dordrecht: Springer, 2013), pp.173–93.

Tuck, Eve and K. Wayne Yang. 'Decolonization Is Not a Metaphor', *Decolonization: Indigeneity, Education & Society* 1.1 (2012), 1–40.

Wansink, Bjorn, Sanne Akkerman, Itzél Zuiker, and Theo Wubbels. 'Where Does Teaching Multiperspectivity in History Education Begin and End? An Analysis of the Uses of Temporality', *Theory & Research in Social Education* 46.4 (2018), 495–527.

Williams, Raymond. *Marxism and Literature* (Oxford: Oxford University Press, 1977).

Wood, Denis. *Rethinking the Power of Maps* (New York: Guilford Press, 2010).

Digital Resources

Bardic Poetry Database: www.bardic.celt.dias.ie.
CAIN: www.cain.ulster.ac.uk/index.html.
Corpus of Electronic Texts (CELT): www.celt.ucc.ie.

Champlain Map: www.umaine.edu/canam/publications/champlain-maptheywould-not-take-me-there.
Clifford M. Clucas: www.cliffordmclucas.info/deep-mapping.html.
Collaborative Media Advocacy Platform (CMAP): www.cmapping.net.
Dictionary of Irish Biography: www.dib.ie.
Léamh: www.léamh.org.
Logainm: www.logainm.ie.
MACMORRIS: www.macmorris.maynoothuniversity.ie/.
People Live Here: www.people-live-here.org/.
Progressive Geographies: www.progressivegeographies.com/2010/11/04/place-research-network/.
The Statutes Project: www.statutes.org.uk.

Cambridge Elements

Digital Literary Studies

Katherine Bode
Australian National University

Katherine Bode is Professor of Literary and Textual Studies at the Australian National University. Her research explores the critical potential and limitations of computational approaches to literature, in publications including *A World of Fiction: Digital Collections and the Future of Literary History* (2018), *Advancing Digital Humanities: Research, Methods, Theories* (2014), *Reading by Numbers: Recalibrating the Literary Field* (2012), and *Resourceful Reading: The New Empiricism, eResearch and Australian Literary Culture* (2009).

Adam Hammond
University of Toronto

Adam Hammond is Assistant Professor of English at the University of Toronto. He is author of *Literature in the Digital Age* (Cambridge 2016) and co-author of *Modernism: Keywords* (2014). He works on modernism, digital narrative, and computational approaches to literary style. He is editor of the forthcoming *Cambridge Companion to Literature in the Digital Age* and *Cambridge Critical Concepts: Literature and Technology*.

Gabriel Hankins
Clemson University

Gabriel Hankins is Associate Professor of English at Clemson University. His first book is *Interwar Modernism and the Liberal World Order* (Cambridge 2019). He writes on modernism, digital humanities, and color. He is technical manager for the Twentieth Century Literary Letters Project and co-editor on *The Digital Futures of Graduate Study in the Humanities* (in progress).

Advisory Board

David Bammen *University of California, Berkeley*
Amy Earhardt *Texas A&M University*
Dirk Van Hulle *University of Oxford*
Fotis Jannidis *Julius-Maximilians-Universität*
Matthew Kirschenbaum *University of Maryland*
Laura Mandell *Texas A&M University*
Élika Ortega-Guzman *University of Colorado, Boulder*
Marisa Parham *Amherst College*
Rita Raley *University of California, Santa Barbara*
Scott Rettberg *University of Bergen*
Roopika Risam *Salem State University*
Glenn Roe *Sorbonne University*
Whitney Trettien *University of Pennsylvania*
Ted Underwood *University of Illinois*

About the Series

Our series provides short exemplary texts that address a pressing research question of clear scholarly interest within a defined area of literary studies, clearly articulate the method used to address the question, and demonstrate the literary insights achieved.

Cambridge Elements

Digital Literary Studies

Elements in the Series

Can We Be wrong? The Problem of Textual Evidence in a Time of Data
Andrew Piper

Literary Geographies in Balzac and Proust
Melanie Conroy

The Shapes of Stories: Sentiment Analysis for Narrative
Katherine Elkins

Actual Fictions: Literary Representation and Character Network Analysis
Roel Smeets

The Challenges of Born-Digital Fiction: Editions, Translations, and Emulations
Dene Grigar and Mariusz Pisarski

New Approaches for Digital Literary Mapping: Chronotopic Cartography
Sally Bushell and Rebecca Hutcheon

Gender and Literary Geography
Elizabeth F. Evans and Matthew Wilkens

Decolonial Deep Mapping
Patricia Palmer, Evan Bourke and Philip Mac a' Ghoill

A full series listing is available at: www.cambridge.org/EDLS

For EU product safety concerns, contact us at Calle de José Abascal, 56–1º,
28003 Madrid, Spain or eugpsr@cambridge.org.